Rapture

A REWARD FOR READINESS

FOR IN SUCH AN HOUR AS YE THINK NOT,
THE SON OF MAN COMETH.

MATTHEW 24:44

Ray Brubaker

DR. RAY BRUBAKER

Unless otherwise indicated, all scripture quotations are taken from the King James Version of the Bible.

RAPTURE
A Reward For Readiness

Copyright ©2003
Dr. Ray Brubaker

Published by:
GOD'S NEWS BEHIND THE NEWS
BOX 10475, ST. PETERSBURG, FL 33733

ISBN Number: 1-931600-41-4

FOREWORD

What you are about to read is going to stay with you for the rest of your life. It will challenge you to re-examine what you believe. It will force you to think about preconceived notions with a new perspective. As you read these pages, ask God to open your eyes and heart, and prepare you with readiness for the Lord's return.

Ray Brubaker is not merely my Dad, although he is that, he is also a Father in the Faith, to me as well as many other young ministers of the Gospel. He has given his life, now 80 years young, to pave a highway of holiness and readiness for us to follow. The torch that I now carry, to proclaim the soon return of Christ, was handed to me by Ray Brubaker.

As you read this book, you, too, will by handed that same torch of truth.

This book is a compilation of the most important truths that God has ever shared with Ray. It represents the "heart" of this man's message. I pray that what you receive from this book will open your heart as well. May every reader of this book become a faithful witness to the message that Dad has carried to the world, "Jesus is coming soon, be ready".

Dr. Joe VanKoevering

DEDICATION

This book is dedicated to

my dearly, departed wife,

Darlene Brubaker,

the "First Lady of Bible Prophecy"

with whom I shared

this same vision with

for over 55 years,

❧

Dr. Ray Brubaker

TABLE OF CONTENTS

INTRODUCTION
SIGNS OF THE TIMES

The prophetic events of today indicate that we are very close to the end of time. In Matthew 24:6, the scripture talks about "wars and rumors of wars"; as we see this coming to pass, even now.

When Jesus was on earth His disciples came to Him privately to ask: "What shall be the sign of thy coming, and of the end of the world?" Our Lord responded to their question with this warning - "Take heed that no man deceive you!"

There is much deception abroad as countless voices are crying for a listening ear. Cults, Isms, and Sects flourish, oftentimes relying on prophecy to propagate their false doctrine.

Also, there is much confusion in relation to the coming of Jesus – when He will come – whether before the tribulation, after the tribulation, or in the middle of the tribulation. This confusion stems largely from a lack of proper interpretation of the Word of God under the guidance of the Holy Spirit who promises to lead us into all truth. May we be assured that there will be no errors or mistakes if we are tuned in to the wavelength of the voice of the Spirit of God who is the author of the Word and the one who interprets that Word to our hearts.

It is with love for our Lord's soon appearing, and not for the sake of controversy, that we write the following chapters which are not meant to be an exhaustive commentary on the subjects under discussion, but rather to give a sense of direction as we seek to understand God's Word. May we be assured that we will always be right if our faith rests on what God has to say rather than what man writes or says.

Remember, take heed that no man deceive you. Man may deceive, but God will never deceive us for He has given us a sure Word of prophecy. When attending the International Congress on Prophecy in New York City in 1955, we were led largely as a result of that meeting to launch our worldwide broadcast. The meeting was held at Calvary Baptist Church.

One of the speakers was Dr. Wilbur Smith who was my teacher while I was a student at Moody Bible Institute. He is perhaps the most learned prophetic scholar of our day whose life has been given to a research of the Scriptures and writings of other Biblical scholars.

On this occasion, Dr. Smith stressed this important consideration that "Prophetic study is useless unless it develops a greater love for Jesus, and holiness of life." Noted Smith, "One can study prophecy and be out of the will of God."

We readily admit the dangers which we see in the discussion of prophecy and do not wish to fall victim to any of these errors or entanglements. We would not knowingly or willingly be guilty of "handling the Word of God deceitfully." (Colossians 4:2) For that reason we would like to call attention to some of the cautions of Scripture.

First, there is the danger of mis-interpretation-adding to or taking from the Word of God. In Revelation 22:18-19 we read: "For I testify unto every man that heareth the words of the prophecy of this book, If any man shall add unto these things, God shall add unto him the plagues that are written in this book: And if any man shall take away from the words of the book of this prophecy, God shall take away his part Out of the book of life, and out of the holy City, and from the things which are written in this book."

Do you understand how with fear and trembling we approach our study, not with personal dogmatism asserting our beliefs, but with a desire to speak, "Thus saith the Lord."

The only safe position is to seek to present the Word of God and when we give an interpretation, to label it as our own personal view. With this in mind we want to make clear that this presentation is our interpretation following years of study based upon the Word of God. And God promises to bless His Word reminding us it will not return void.

In the second place, there is this common danger of injecting our own thoughts into our message. We seek to avoid this danger. We do not want to be bound by tradition, denominational bias, doctrinal beliefs, but solely responsible to the clear teaching of the Word of God.

The Apostle Peter, when expressing his own view and opinion, found the Lord turning to him to say, "Get thee behind me, Satan for thou savourest not the things that be of God but be of men!" (Matthew 16:23)

There are other dangers in dealing with prophetic subjects; the danger of promoting one's self or one's opinions rather than exalting Christ. With Paul we would declare, "For we preach not ourselves, but Christ Jesus the Lord; and ourselves your servants for Jesus' sake." (2 Corinthians 4:5)

Then there is the danger of having wrong motives, seeking financial gain or advancing one's reputation. I know from past experience it will cause some to reject this message; for there are those who chose to follow preconceived notions rather than make a diligent study for themselves concerning the truth of God's Word.

I would hope all may have an open mind and an open heart to deal honestly with the Scriptures I seek to discuss realizing I will be held responsible, not to men, but to God, in the day when I stand before the Lord.

Thus, my sole purpose in this book is that we may receive the Word which is able to save our souls and then have an abundant entrance into the presence of Our Lord and Saviour, being welcomed with joy and not with grief, hearing His words, "Well done, thou good and faithful servant, enter thou into the joy of thy Lord!"

CHAPTER 1
WHAT ARE WE FACING?

Dr. Louis Talbot writes: "I believe the human imagination is absolutely incapable of picturing the awful days of the tribulation period. It will be the most awful time ever known, because it will be the first time the devil will be allowed to exercise such power. There will be signs in the heavens above and on the earth beneath. Great catastrophes like the one that once made of San Francisco a heap of ruins will be repeated, only on a far greater scale. The centers of a boasted civilization with the foundation of blood and tears will crumble to the ground. Intense heat will burn the grass and trees of the field. Pestilences like bubonic plague will carry off thousands. The sun will be darkened; the moon turned into blood; the stars of heaven will not give their light. It will be such a time of trouble as never was, "No, nor ever shall be."

Now, the question we might ask – Will believers on earth at this time of unparalleled lawlessness have to suffer the consequence of the judgment seen pronounced upon the wicked? Will the Church have to go through the tribulation?

What did Paul mean when on account of man's rebellion against God there is this pronouncement of "Tribulation and anguish, upon every soul of man that doeth evil, of the Jew first, and also of the Gentile; But glory, honour, and peace, to every man that worketh good, to the Jew first, and also to the Gentile." Romans 3:9-10

Tribulation is the due of evil doers, And such tribulation such as the world has never seen, nor ever shall see again, said Jesus.

No wonder, Dr. V. Raymond Edman, former Chancellor of Wheaton College, has said: "The day of the Lord will bring the greatest tribulation ever experienced by this bewildered and bruised old world. As earth's first civilization declined into the unspeakable godlessness and wickedness of the days of Noah, so will the coming of the day of the Lord."

Dr. Oswald J. Smith notes: "Earth's darkest hour lies just ahead!" Dr. Smith, incidentally, believes the Church will go through this dark, dismal age of unparalleled death and destruction we call the tribulation period.

In his first book on prophecy, Dr. Smith wrote: "I have always held the view that the Rapture precedes the Revelation by some seven years, and that the Church, therefore, will not go through the Tribulation, but I do not want to be dogmatic about it and, if God should reveal the contrary to me, I will gladly accept it!"

I have great admiration for Dr. Smith and would hope everyone of the readers of this book would have the same open mind to the truth of God's Word.

However, Dr. Smith did eventually change his position. He writes: "Now, after years of study and prayer, I am absolutely convinced that there will be no rapture before the tribulation, but that the Church will undoubtedly be called upon to face the Antichrist, and that Christ will come at the close and not at the beginning of that awful period."

Let us look into the Word of God to see what will transpire during this tribulation time. Then, ask ourselves the question whether we would be able to endure this time of trouble just ahead.

It would appear that the Tribulation dawns with the rise of Antichrist who will demand that all receive a mark of identification. Without this no man can buy or sell. Stop and think for a moment. Just how important is your Social Security card or bank card? If now receiving the benefits of a monthly check, you would certainly not want to give up your card without a protest. "Where will I get enough money to buy groceries and pay my rent?" would be your cry.

Similarly, to refuse this mark of identification required for all, will find one unable to purchase food or clothing, and unable to sell any produce or possessions.

How long would a person resist such a system? There are many today who follow the fads and fashions because they feel they have to go along with the crowd, whatever society may dictate. You can be sure these same people would fall for the Antichrist program if they can't say "no" to the temptation to be different. During the Tribulation there will be a one-world, religious-political empire, and to refuse loyalty to this system will bring death.

How many will have the courage that it takes to be different then, if they can't withstand the pressure to be different now?

Then the Tribulation will be characterized by unspeakable woes, horrors, and judgments. Famine and pestilence will follow devastating wars and great earthquakes. There will be thunderings and lightnings rocking heaven and earth. Stars will fall from Heaven upon the earth making the waters bitter, and great hail weighing 55 to 100 pounds will not be uncommon. The sun shall scorch men with great heat before they suffer the judgment of darkness. Gross darkness shall cover the earth as the moon, too, shall become dark.

Another star is seen falling to the earth and the concussion splits open the earth, and the Bible describes the appearance of creatures like locusts with the ability to torment men five months. Their torment was like that of a scorpion when he striketh a man. Those bitten will wish they could die, but can't.

Noisome and grievous sores appear on the world's inhabitants, and they blaspheme the God of Heaven because of their pains and sores. The sea becomes as the blood of a dead man and all living things die. Amidst powerful earthquakes, mountains are leveled and the islands disappear into the sea. Besides all the judgments herein described, we read of Satan himself actually dwelling upon the earth, ruling through his puppet, the Antichrist!

The imagination cannot begin to describe conditions that will then prevail. Mark reminds us, "Then shall be great AFFLICTION!" Noisome and grievous sores will afflict all who take the mark of the beast, and great pain will cause men to gnaw their tongues and blaspheme the God of Heaven. Paul tells us the day of the Lord will be as the travail of a woman with child from which there is no escape!

No escape! Those will be sad words to fall upon the ears of many whose fate will be a kind of hell on earth. For the tribulation is one awful time of sorrow from which there will be no escape once it comes.

However, we cannot help but believe there is escape from this awful holocaust seen coming upon the world. For, did not our Lord urge His disciples, saying: "Watch ye therefore, and pray always, that ye may be accounted worthy to escape all these things that shall come to pass, and to stand before the Son of man!"

Would our Lord hold out the possibility of escape if there were no escape? Did He not indicate the possibility of escaping "all these things" that shall come to pass? That this promise of "escape" is conditioned upon our faithful watching and praying is certainly implied here. So, let no one rest solely upon their decision for Christ that they may have made years or days ago. Rather, we are given explicit orders to make preparation for the day of Christ's appearing. A wedding is about to be consummated, and it cannot be that there isn't the necessary preparation. In fact, we read: "His wife hath made herself ready. And to her was granted that she should be arrayed in fine linen, clean and white: for the fine linen is the righteousness of saints." Revelation 19:7-8.

As Sarah Foulkes Moore, former editor of the HERALD OF HIS COMING publication, sums it up: "All the Lord's emphatic warnings in His many parables in Matthew 24 and 25 are exhortations to uninterrupted watchfulness. He gave His disciples no reason to believe their readiness for the Rapture rested on any experience of salvation that they may have had. He made it pointed and plain that their conduct at the moment of the Rapture meant the winning of the prize. All teaching, all reaching, all activity, religious, secular, or otherwise that today ignores the Lord's solemn warning to His own to 'watch and pray always that ye may be accounted worthy' dissipates watchfulness and makes for sloth and carelessness."

Thus should be the believer's encouragement to watchfulness, prayerfulness and faithfulness. May we be reminded that the very nature of the word "Church" implies a select company of saints that will be caught up to meet the Lord in the air at the Rapture. For the word "Church" is the Greek word "Ekklesia" which means "called-out" ones.

While we may have assurance of our salvation which rests upon the Word of God and the Spirit's witness to our own heart, let us not become lukewarm in our Christian experience, but ever live in constant expectancy and readiness for that all-glorious event.

Again quoting Mrs. Moore: "Christ made ever-pressing the necessity of being ever ready. It is not without intent that He left the time of His Advent unknown in order to keep us in a constant state of instant readiness." Thus, this constitutes our message. We would urge immediate steps be taken to come to a knowledge of such readiness that will find us escaping the coming judgment seen befalling the world. By trusting Christ as our Saviour and Lord, having renounced a life of sin through faith in His shed blood to cover past sin, and then by living daily for Christ through the help of the Holy Spirit, we can be ready for rapture!

For our Lord has urged us, saying: "Be ye ready also, for in such an hour as ye think not, the Son of man cometh!"

CHAPTER 2
ARE YOU READY FOR THE RAPTURE?

Suppose you had never seen a copy of the Bible, but you became stranded on an island where you came upon a copy of the precious Word of God for the very first time. Would you believe as you do today?

Our belief in the Scriptures is often flavored by our past traditions—how we were taught the Bible in our youth, or in our churches and colleges, or our acceptance of the views of theologians of the past. Thus some proclaim they are Calvinists, while others say they're Armenians, or Wesleyans or Pentecostals.

I covet your interest in a study of the Word of God with an open mind and without prejudice, and believe I see evidence of all of these views expressed in the Scriptures. Now, in the same way, I would like to approach my study of the rapture. Regardless of your belief, why not accept the verdict of Holy Scripture?

I admit the word "rapture" is not in the Bible. Webster's primary definition of the word is the "act of transporting, or fact of being transported," and relates to our Lord's return for His own.

The history of belief in a "rapture," according to some, began with a woman who stood up in Edward Irving's church in London, in 1831, claiming a special revelation that the Church would be removed before the coming awful tribulation. Although this woman was what we might call "Pentecostal" in that she claimed divine revelation, her teaching was quickly adopted by J. N. Darby of the Plymouth Brethren movement, and later by C. I. Scofield who popularized the view.

To us it is strange that many evangelicals who follow the Scofield Bible will have nothing to do with "Pentecostals" although they accept the idea of a "rapture" reported to have come from a revelation given Margaret MacDonald.

It is likewise strange that some of today's Pentecostals who accept divine revelation through "tongues" and "interpretation of tongues" do not hold any longer to a belief in a pre-tribulation rapture, or any rapture.

For that reason, our only safe guide must be the Word of God. In this study I would seek to emphasize:

(1) Our belief in the rapture occurring before the tribulation;

(2) Our belief that many anticipating rapture will miss this event to go through the tribulation; and

(3) Our listing of possible errors surrounding a belief in the rapture.

There are too many evangelicals like Scofield, Ben Newton, M. R. DeHaan, Charles Fuller, and names too numerous to mention who believed and taught that all believers, carnal and spiritual, will be caught up at the rapture before the coming tribulation. Then there are those men as Henry Frost of the China Inland Mission, William and Charles Erdman, Dr. Carl F. Henry, Harold Ockenga, and Robert McQuilken who believe that the Church will go through the tribulation.

We believe the Scriptures teach that there is an event we call the rapture. For I Thessalonians 4 relates the coming of the Lord, at which time, we shall be "caught up" to meet Him in the air, if we are ready.

In the second place, the promise is to those "in Christ" (I Thessalonians 4:16) which we know are those who are born again, that they shall participate in this glorious event. For remember, "If a man be IN CHRIST, he is a new creature..." (2 Corinthians 5:17). Pardon my saying so, but many who claim to be born again, according to the Scriptures, are not. Read I John 3:9 and I John 5:18 and see if you have this born-again experience and no longer practice sin.

Finally, I'm convinced the rapture will reveal that those who will be ready are only a small group out of the vast majority of believers who professed to be looking for Christ's return. The call of the Lord to all of us is to "watch and pray always, that ye may be accounted worthy to escape all these things that shall come to pass, and to stand before the Son of man." (Luke 21:36) I would note that this promise of escape is conditioned upon faithful watching and praying that we will escape. Perhaps in some parts of the world they are praying for release from tortures being endured for their faith in Christ, and they shall escape in answer to prayer. Although I may not be so tortured for Christ, I should ever be constantly praying, "Even so, come quickly, Lord Jesus,"

As an umpire in baseball calls the balls and strikes fairly as he sees them, so I have prepared this study for you to read, study and evaluate. I do not come with dogmatic argument, but with prayerful consideration of this doctrine, which should cause all of us to want to live closer to our Lord. Like Enoch, may we be found "walking with God" and then suddenly find our communion and fellowship drawing us into the very presence of our Lord at His coming.

CHAPTER 3
MAKE THE RAPTURE YOUR GOAL!

How many times I have asked my audience..."How many want to be in the First Resurrection?"

In Revelation 20:4 we read:"I saw the souls of them that were beheaded for the witness of Jesus, and for the word of God, and which had not worshipped the beast, neither his image, neither had received his mark upon their foreheads, or in their hands; and they lived and reigned with Christ a thousand years. But the rest of the dead lived not again until the thousand years was finished. THIS IS THE FIRST RESURRECTION!

Do you want to be in that era when Antichrist rules and requires all to identify with his system by taking the 666 mark, and then beheaded for your refusal to do so?

We continue to read:"Blessed and holy is he that hath part in the first resurrection: on such the second death hath no power; but they shall be priests of God and of Christ, and shall reign with him a thousand years!"

What is the explanation for this? For according to this scripture the First Resurrection doesn't occur until after the seven years of tribulation seen coming upon the world when Antichrist rules and requires all identify with his system of world government, bow down and worship him, accepting his mark of 666, or upon refusal to do all this will be beheaded.

The Apostle Paul would seem to explain that he was not looking to be in that First Resurrection. That's why in Philippians 3:10-11 he explains,"That I may know him, and the power of his resurrection, and the fellowship of his sufferings, being made conformable unto his death. If by any means I might attain unto the resurrection of the dead."

Now you almost need to know and understand the original

Greek text to know what the Apostle Paul was saying.

A.T. Robertson, noted Greek Scholar, would seem to indicate Paul knew in God's plan the event we call the First Resurrection would take place at the climax of the tribulation period and just preceding the Kingdom Age when our Lord reigns for a thousand year.

Paul is not looking for that First Resurrection. Rather, as Robertson explains, "Apparently Paul is thinking only believers out from the dead," as if he doesn't expect to be in that resurrection which in the plan of God occurs at the end of the tribulation, and just before the kingdom age. Rather, he has revelation that it is possible to escape being in that First Resurrection, for an earlier event I call the Rapture, which also finds those who will be resurrected.

Or, as my Greek teacher, Dr. Kenneth Wuest, in WORD PICTURES, Volume 4, page 454 explains, Paul is saying, "If by any means I may advance to the earlier resurrection which is from among the dead."

Charles Fuller, of the Old Fashioned Revival Hour, calls this resurrection spoken of by Paul, and including the Rapture, as being "the first part of the First Resurrection".

Would you believe the Apostle Paul questioned whether he would be in that earlier resurrection or rapture, explaining, "Not as though I had already attained, either were already perfect; but I follow after, if that it may apprehend that for which also I am apprehended of Christ Jesus." Again Paul repeats, "Brethren, I count not myself to have apprehended; but this one thing I do, forgetting those things which are behind and reaching forth unto those things which are before, I press toward the mark of the prize of the high calling of God in Christ Jesus."

Not until the end of his life could the Apostle Paul say, "For now I am ready to be offered, and the time of my departure is at hand. I have fought a good fight, I have finished my course, I have kept the faith; Henceforth there is laid up of me a crown of righteousness, which the Lord, the righteous judge, shall give me at that day; and not to me only, but unto all them also that love his appearing."

The Apostle Paul values the prize of the high calling of God, or what the original text states the upward call, as something which he hopes the Lord would find him worthy, and which he concludes all can be worthy if we love our Lord's appearing

Writing to Titus, the Apostle Paul speaks of the demand to deny ungodliness, and worldly lusts, living soberly, righteously and godly in this present world, "Looking for that Blessed Hope, and the glorious appearing of the great God and our Saviour Jesus Christ; Who gave himself for us that he might redeem us from all iniquity, and purify unto himself a peculiar people zealous of good works."

The Apostle John likewise calls attention to Christ's coming, saying: "when he shall appear, we shall be like him; for we shall se him as He is. And every man that hath this hope in him purifieth himself, even as he is pure." 1 John 3:2-3

Jude quotes Enoch as saying, "Behold the Lord cometh with ten thousands of his saints." That's quite a contrast to those who speak of millions being raptured. Dave Hunt, in his writings pictured 1.7 billion who call themselves Christians, but he sees only a fraction of that number being raptured.

The Laodicean Church Age is said to describe the period of time just before the Rapture where the Lord says, "I know thy works that thou are neither cold nor hot, I will spue thee out of my mouth. Because thou sayest, I am rich, and increased with goods, and have need of nothing; and knowest not that thou art wretched, and miserable, and poor, and blind and naked;" Revelation 3:15-17

Now some would have us believe that all of these Laodiceans are professing believers who will be "spued out", left behind at the Rapture. However, our Lord says, "As many as I love, I rebuke and chasten, be zealous therefore and repent." Revelation 3:19

In Hebrews 12:6 we read, "For whom the Lord loveth he chasteneth, and scourgeth every son whom he receiveth." So there must be those believers among the Laodiceans and they are left behind at the rapture to go through the tribulation which would be a time of chastening for them.

On the other hand, the Philadelphia Church representing those who keep the Word of God, the Lord promises to keep them from the hour of temptation, or the tribulation, which shall come upon all the world. The tribulation will be a testing time which God has determined to find out whether believers will fall for the antichrist doctrine, accept his mark, and as a result they forfeit eternal life, proving they were not truly born again in the first place.

Revelation 7:9 describes "a great multitude, which no man could number, of all nations, and kindreds, and people, and tongues, standing before the throne, and before the Lamb, clothed with white robes and palms in their hands."

We read, one of the elders asks, "What are these which are arrayed in white robes, and whence came they?"

The answer is heard, "Sir, thou knowest...These are they which came out of great tribulation, and have washed their robes, and made them white in the blood of the Lamb."

In Revelation 22:14, in the last chapter of your Bible, we read: "Blessed are they that do his commandments, that they may have right to the tree of life." Actually the translators should have used the original Greek text which reads, "Blessed are they that wash their robes..."

Like at Sardis, we read of those which had not defiled their garments, and they shall walk with me in white, for they are worthy!"

We have come to accept the interpretation that this great multitude seen coming through the tribulation, and seen washing their robes, represent the converts found accepting Christ during the tribulation, the result of the preaching of the 144,000 converted Jews.

However, this is the time of the Jews greatest persecution, known of as the "time of Jacob's trouble" where Jews will be fleeing to the mountains where they will be protected by God, and its doubtful whether they could survive the persecution of witnessing on the streets of their home town and cities. Thus, instead of millions being raptured the possibility exists that millions will be left behind at the Rapture, and faced with the decision to take the mark of the antichrist or be beheaded, they will choose to die for Jesus Christ, and will be a part of the First Resurrection that occurs seven years after the Rapture.

We know the Laodiceans will no doubt make up that great multitude which no man could number, who will be beheaded.

Whereas, James and John, who came to Jesus and asked him, "Grant to us that we may sit on thy right hand, and the other on thy left hand, in thy glory," the Lord replied, "to sit on my right hand and on my left hand is not mine to give, but it shall be given to them for whom it is prepared.

To the Laodiceans, who are spued out into the tribulation, if they do not identify with the Antichrist, and remain true to Jesus Christ, and thus die for their faith, our Lord promises, "To him that overcometh will I grant to sit with me in my throne, even as I also overcame, and am set down with my Father in his throne." (Revelation 3:21)

If left behind at the Rapture this will be opportunity to

prove ones faith in Jesus Christ, for willingness to die for Jesus Christ is the greatest testimony of ones faith. Thus; we read, "Blessed and holy is he that hath part in the first resurrection; on such the second death hath no power, but they shall be priests of God and of Christ, and shall reign with him a thousand years!"

Left behind at the Rapture is not without its reward for all who remain faithful to Jesus Christ. It surely is worth living for Jesus Christ and being raptured when He comes but for those left behind this can become their most glorious hour by dying for their Lord and then reigning with Him when He comes into His kingdom.

Is the Rapture your goal?

Are you looking for Christ's Return?

Are you ready were He to come today?

If the Apostle Paul questioned his readiness for the Rapture, which is what we see scholars saying he meant, then what about us? How ready are we for this all-glorious event?

Hudson Taylor once wrote, "We wish to place on record our solemn conviction that not all who are Christians or think themselves to be such, will attain to that resurrection of which St. Paul speaks in Philippians 3:12."

Likewise C. Campbell Morgan, commenting on the great multitude seen coming through the Great Tribulation, and found washing their robes and making them white in the blood of the Lamb, comments: "Personally, I am convinced that not all Christian people will be taken to be with Christ on His Return, but only those who by the attitude of their lives are ready for His appearance." In 1 John 2:28 we have the Apostle John saying, "And now, little children, abide in him; that, when he shall appear, we may have confidence, and not be ashamed at his coming."

Dr. Kenneth Wuest notes the word "ashamed" is better

translated, "in shame shrink back from Him." Vincent, the Greek scholar agrees, saying: "The fundamental thought is that of separation and shrinking from God through the shame of conscious guilt." C. Campbell Morgan notes, "The picture is that of persons so conscious of unreadiness that they dare not face Him. The root meaning of the word 'ashamed' is "disgraced", so that it is allowable to read, "and not be disgraced from Him at His coming." Morgan points out, "This is not addressed to the outside world, but to the believer in Christ. In that verse there is a very clear division which, to my mind, answers the question whether believers may not pass through the great tribulation. Some will be ready to enjoy freedom of access to Christ and familiarity with Him; but the 'little children' of Cod who have been living only in the elements of the world will be disgraced at His appearing."

Then states Morgan, "Those who are abiding in Christ here on earth, who purify themselves as He is pure, separated ones cut clean adrift from the ungodliness of the age, loyal of heart to the King in the days of waiting for Him -these are the men and women who will have boldness in the day of His coming." Then asks Morgan, "Who shall draw the line?" He replies, "I do not," adding, "It is for each of us to make application of this truth in solitude."

To be left behind at the Rapture is not an indication one is not saved. Rather, it indicates one was not ready for that glorious event. In Revelation 19:7-8 we read, "Let us be glad and rejoice and give honour to him; for the marriage of the Lamb is come, and His wife hath made herself ready! And to her was granted that she should be arrayed in fine linen, clean and white; for the fine linen is the righteousness of saints." Notice, this is not the righteousness alone received as a result of our salvation, but implied is when given robes of righteousness we are to keep them clean, with the fine linen representing the "righteous deeds" of the saints. (See Revised Standard and other versions.)

It is clearly taught believers in-Christ should anticipate the Rapture. Paul, writing to the Thessalonians notes, "For if we believe that Jesus died and rose again, even so them also which sleep in Jesus will God bring with him." (1 Thessalonians 4:14) And again we read, "For God hath not appointed us to wrath, but to obtain salvation by our Lord Jesus Christ." (1 Thessalonians 5:9)

However, in Ephesians 5, writing to believers, Paul warns, "But fornication and all uncleanness, or covetousness, let it not be once named among you, as becometh saints; Neither filthiness, nor foolish talking, nor jesting, which are not convenient, but rather giving of thanks. For this ye know, that no whoremonger, nor unclean person, nor covetous man, who is an idolater, hath any inheritance in the kingdom of Christ and of God." Writes Paul, "Let no man deceive you with vain words; for because of these things cometh the WRATH OF GOD upon the children of disobedience. Be not ye therefore partakers with them" (Ephesians 5:1-7) M.R. DeHaan of the Radio Bible Class wrote, "Let me seriously warn you that God wants His people clean. The Lord will not tolerate a defiled bride. God help us to examine ourselves and make ourselves ready now!"

In Matthew and in Luke's gospel we have the parable of the marriage feast with the announcement, "The wedding is ready, but they which were bidden were not worthy." Throughout eternity our song shall be, Worthy is the Lamb!

However, when it comes to the Rapture did not our Lord command, "WATCH YE THEREFORE and pray always that ye may be accounted worthy to escape all these things that shall come to pass and to stand before the SON OF MAN?" (Luke 21:36)

We take for granted because we made a decision for Christ we are automatically ready for the Rapture whenever it occurs. However, as Lot's wife was given command not to look back on Sodom and turned into a pillar of salt, so we are given command to pray that we may be accounted worthy to escape all of the things spoken of to take place in days ahead. In fact, I don't think we should have seen 9/11 in New York City for that could have been avoided were we to follow our Lord's command. Witnessing these coming events should find us praying, "Come Lord Jesus! Come Quickly!" believing He is ready and waiting to come. He awaits our prayer of command.

In the parable of the Wedding Supper there appeared a man without a wedding garment. He was taken and carried away and cast into outer darkness, where there is weeping and gnashing of teeth.

John Wesley, asked about this garment, stated that garment is "holiness".

How is it we don't have more emphasis on sanctification and holiness? In 2 Thessalonians 2:13 we read, "God hath from the beginning chosen you to salvation through sanctification of the Spirit and belief of the truth."

We accept the truth of the Gospel which brings about our salvation, but why do we not hear messages on sanctification and holiness?

As D. M. Panton once wrote, "The Holy Son of God cannot present unto HIMSELF a trifling, indifferent, unsanctified body of nominal church members. His church must be made like unto Himself, the fairest and noblest expression of redeemed humanity that only His sufferings and death could ever produce." In Ephesians 5:26 & 27 God's purpose is to sanctify and cleanse us by the Word, "That He might present to Himself a glorious church, not having spot, or wrinkle, or any such thing; but that it should be holy and without blemish."

John Calvin related, "Whosoever therefore wishes to persist in the course of a sanctified life must hold fast to hope in the Return of Christ!" And, Dr. A. Skevington Wood declared, "Holiness stimulates hope!"

In Hebrews 12:16 are we not admonished, "Follow peace with all men, and holiness, without which no man shall see the Lord."

When it comes to the Rapture in connection with the man without a wedding garment our Lord concludes, "For many are called, but few are chosen." (Matthew 22: 14)

Whereas, in Revelation 17:14 where our Lord is seen coming from heaven, as King of kings and Lord of lords we read, "They that are with Him are called, chosen and faithful!" If wanting to be in the rapture it would appear this should be our description, "For we are a chosen generation, a royal priesthood, an holy nation, a peculiar people...CALLED out of darkness into His marvelous light. (I Peter 2:9) Then we are CHOSEN IN Him before the foundation of the world, that we should be holy and without blame before Him in love. And finally, in such passages as 1 Timothy 6:2 we have those described as FAITHFUL and beloved, or in Revelation 2:10 where we read, "Be thou faithful unto death, and I will give thee a crown of life."

Are we among the CALLED, CHOSEN & FAITHFUL?

I might quote Walt Dumont who writes, "The current popular teaching is that all Christians will attain to the rapture. But that's not what Jesus and Paul taught. Jesus explained that the Holy Spirit filled believers who trimmed their lamps would be accepted by the bridegroom. (Matthew 25:1-13).

He points out, "The foolish virgins didn't make the rapture! Contemporary theologians assume the foolish virgins to be unsaved people" But of the foolish virgins we read, "Our lamps are going out." (Matthew 25:8b) He explains, "In other words, their lamps were still feebly burning... and in the process of going out, and insufficiently lit to meet the bridegroom."

Dumont explains, "Oil always represents the Holy Spirit." Jesus said of the Holy Spirit, He dwelleth with you and shall be in you." (John 14:17) Of this we can be certain, "the wise took oil in their vessels with their lamps." And, also when the bridegroom came it was said, "and they that were ready went in with him to the marriage and the door was shut." (Matthew 25:10)

I conclude by quoting Matthew 24:44, "Therefore be ye also ready: for in such an hour as ye think not the Son of man cometh."

CHAPTER 4
THE RAPTURE QUESTION

Queen Elizabeth II, on her "official birthday," honored J. S. Jones, a postman in North Wales. In selecting Jones to receive the British Empire Medal, she noted he was a member of a family that has delivered the Welsh mail for 150 years. Upon conferring an award upon Jones, age 60, she noted he had "not missed a day's service in 43 years." Also, he "got the mail through despite snow, storms and floods."

Is this not a reminder of the day when Christ shall REWARD ALL WHO ARE FAITHFUL IN His service? As we read in Matthew 16:26, "For the Son of Man shall come in the glory of His Father with his angels, and then he shall reward every man according to his works."

We are not saved by works. As we're reminded in Ephesians 2:8-9, we are saved "by grace, through faith...not of works, lest any man should boast." However, being saved, we are enjoined to be "zealous of good works" and also to "be careful to maintain good works."

Dr. Wilbur Smith once related that very few books have ever been published relating to the believer's works. And yet, at least 18 times "works" is mentioned in the book of Revelation alone.

For instance, we read: "Behold, I come quickly; and my reward is with me, to give every man according as his work shall be." (Revelation 22:12)

Then we are told of four classifications of those to be rewarded. For we read: "He that is unjust, let him be unjust still: and he which is filthy, let him be filthy still: and he that is righteous, let him be righteous still, and he that is holy, let him be holy still." (verse 11)

We usually think of a person as being saved or unsaved.

But when it comes to rewarding according to our works, we find four classifications of men.

Some may not agree, but their disagreement is with the Bible which clearly reveals these four classifications. Furthermore, each is to be rewarded at the coming of our Blessed Lord.

Let's seek to take a closer look at each group to seek to discover in which class we find ourselves.

CLASSIFICATION NUMBER ONE: THE UNJUST

We know this represents the unsaved - thieves, murderers, liars, gamblers, because we read: "Christ died, the just for the UNJUST" (I Peter 3:18)

What a message is ours to proclaim! No one need to go on in their sin. Christ died for the unjust!

If sinners do not repent and turn to the Lord for salvation, there is only the reward of punishment. As Peter declares: "The Lord knoweth how to deliver the godly out of temptation, but to reserve the UNJUST unto the day of judgment to be punished." (2 Peter 2:9)

It's awful for a child to know he's going to get a whipping. So the sinner who does not repent and receive Jesus faces the coming great day of wrath as well as eternal separation from God in hell.

CLASSIFICATION NUMBER TWO: THE FILTHY

While following a long string of cars on a narrow country road, I noticed a truck pulling a huge derrick up ahead. In the car in front of me the driver must have gotten awfully nervous, for it seemed every 20 seconds he would spit tobacco juice out the window, and some of it came my way. Well, when this happened, I thought of this verse which mentions the "filthy."

Billy Sunday once said, "Tobacco might not keep a man from

heaven, but he sure can't spit there."

Paul, writing to Christians, urges them, saying: "Let us cleanse ourselves from all filthiness of the flesh and spirit, perfecting holiness in the fear of God." (2 Corinthians 7:1)

James similarly urges, "Wherefore lay apart all filthiness." (James 1:21)

Concerning Lot, we read he was "vexed with the filthy conversation of the wicked." (2 Peter 2:7)

How many are vexed with filthiness which may take the form of lying, cheating, hating, anger, greed, selfishness, or intemperance. Or, we think of filthy movies, trashy literature, which some who call themselves Christians patronize.

While it is true that a person that is a Christian may fall victim to temptation, it is also true that on account of filthiness, many are going to be rewarded with the wrath of God at the coming of Jesus. Some say God's wrath will never fall on the believer. Yet in Ephesians we read: "But fornication, and all uncleanness, or covetousness, let it not be once named among you, as becometh saints; neither filthiness, nor foolish talking, nor jesting". Let no man deceive you with vain words: for because of these things cometh the wrath of God upon the children of disobedience, Be not ye therefore partakers with them." (Ephesians 5:3-7)

One noted evangelist declared: "The Bible teaches that God hates immorality as much as, or more than, any other sin."

CLASSIFICATION NUMBER THREE: THE RIGHTEOUS

How wonderful to be included among the righteous - those who have repented of sin to trust the Saviour. The righteous represents the "saved." For we are made righteous as we trust in Christ, receiving forgiveness through His shed blood. We read, "For he hath made him to be sin for us, who knew no sin, that we might be made the righteousness of God in him," (2 Corinthians 5:21)

Let me point out - if we are really RIGHTEOUS, we will be found living righteously when Jesus comes. Writes John: "Little children, let no man deceive you, he that doeth righteousness is righteous even as He is righteous. He that committeth sin is of the devil." (1 John 3:7-8)

When Christ returns and we are among the righteous, shall we not be found rewarded at the rapture? Paul speaks of the "crown of righteousness, which the Lord, the righteous judge, shall give me at that day..." (2 Timothy 4:8)

CLASSIFICATION NUMBER FOUR: THE HOLY

"Blessed and holy is he that hath part in the first resurrection." (Revelation 20:6)

The Greek word for "holy" is Hagiasmos. It is sometimes translated into such words as "saint," "sanctify," "sanctification." Its primary meaning is to be "set apart to God."

Dr. M. R. DeHaan pointed out the difference between being a believer and a disciple, showing the disciple to be one willing to give up all to follow Jesus. Similarly there is a difference between the "righteous" who are the saved, and the "holy" who represent those who are sanctified.

We're reminded of Jesus of whom it is written: "Lo, I come to do thy will, O God...by the which will we are sanctified..." (Hebrews 10:9-10) Not only did our Lord sanctify us by His purchase of each of us when He died on the cross, but when His will becomes our will, then we, too, are sanctified. With some this is a long, drawn-out process before they finally surrender to the total will of God. God will bear witness through the Holy Spirit when we make this unconditional surrender.

Scriptural progression in the Christian life is emphasized in Romans 6:19. Here we read: "...for as ye have yielded your members servants to uncleanness and to iniquity; even so now yield your members servants to righteousness unto holiness." Did you notice the progression?

A child steals a cookie from the cupboard and then tells a lie to cover it up. So in the Christian life there is progression from righteousness unto holiness. It is in view of our Lord's return that we are admonished to pursue this holiness. We read, "Follow peace with all men, and holiness without which no man shall see the Lord."

We might point out, too, that "holiness" is the opposite of "impurity." For we read, "God hath not called us to uncleanness but to holiness." Thus, God's purpose for us is that we be among the righteous and the holy when Jesus comes.

Beloved, let us remember our Lord promises to reward our efforts.

A man at the Buffalo airport handled the baggage for a couple from New Zealand who had just toured the United States. Having purchased a car in Miami, they now had no more need of the vehicle, so they told the skycap - "It's yours?"

What reward for such little effort! And yet the Lord promises to reward our least, little effort.

Is this not an incentive for whole-hearted service? Should we not strive for what we might consider the greatest of all rewards - that of being accepted at our Lord's Coming with the words, "Well done, thou good and faithful servant, enter thou into the joy of thy Lord!"

The Apostle Paul may have had this determination in mind when aspiring to rapture. For he wrote: "Brethren, I count not myself to have apprehended: but this one thing I do, forgetting those things which are before, I press toward the mark for the prize of the high calling of God in Christ Jesus." (Philippians 3:10).

The "high" calling refers to the "upward" calling or what some consider to be "caught upward" at the coming of our Blessed Lord. Remember, in this passage Paul had some question about attaining the resurrection. For he wrote, "If by any means I might attain unto the resurrection of the dead." (verse 11)

Would this not indicate that the resurrection at the rapture was a prize to be gained, even as the crown that would be given to those who love our Lord's appearing?

He admonished in view of His coming, "Watch ye therefore and pray always, that ye may be accounted worthy to escape all these things that shall come to pass, and to stand before the son of man."

Doesn't this give the impression that Rapture is the reward of readiness? Is escape from coming tribulation based on being accounted worthy of escape? This is what our Lord seems to indicate, and this is what Paul seems to be saying. For in 2 Thessalonians, he also speaks of being "accounted worthy of the kingdom of God." And again he writes, "We pray always for you, that our God would count you worthy of this calling...".

So, we would almost conclude by saying...RAPTURE is a reward to be gained...a reward to the faithful who are ready when Christ appears. And we would urge - "Be ye therefore ready also; for in such an hour as ye think not, the son of man cometh!"

CHAPTER 5

OUR LORD'S RETURN…A BLESSED HOPE FOR THOSE WHO ARE READY!

Dr. Herbert Lockyer has declared:"The imminent return of Christ has enabled the believers of each succeeding generation to gather comfort, strength, and inspiration from such a truth. Not knowing the date fixed upon God's Calendar for His beloved Son to come back, the saints are yet upheld by such a blessed hope."

The message of our Lord's Return is meant to be a message of comfort. If we anticipated tribulation rather than rapture, there would be little to comfort us unless we evaluate suffering in the light of eternity. For we do read,"The sufferings of this present time are not worthy to be compared with the glory that shall be revealed in us." (Romans 8:18)

However, it is in view of Paul's marvelous explanation as to how the Lord will come to rapture the saints that we are encouraged, "Wherefore comfort one another with these words." (1 Thessalonians 4:18)

Dr. Ford Philpott relates how one night as he left home for a speaking engagement, his wife requested that he bring a message of comfort. He chose as his text 1 Thessalonians 4:15-18. The words are most familiar to all those who long for the day of Christ's coming. "For this we say unto you by the word of the Lord that we which are alive and remain unto the coming of the Lord shall not prevent them which are asleep. For the Lord himself shall descend from heaven with a shout, with the voice of the archangel, and with the trump of God: and the dead in Christ shall rise first: Then we which are alive and remain shall be caught up together with them in the clouds, to meet the Lord in the air, and so shall we ever be with the Lord. WHEREFORE COMFORT ONE ANOTHER WITH THESE WORDS!"

It must be remembered, however, that to have this hope encourages a close walk with the Lord. It likewise demands forsaking of every known sin, and obedience to the revealed will of God. Even as we read in 1 John 3:3, "And every man that hath this hope in him purifieth himself, even as he is pure."

How does one purify himself? Peter replies: "Seeing you have purified your souls in obeying the truth through the Spirit..." (1 Peter 1:22) But someone asks: "Does not the blood of Jesus cleanse us from all sin and keep us ever ready for the coming of our Blessed Lord?"

The answer comes again from God's Word: "If we walk in the light as He is in the light, we have fellowship one with another, and the blood of Jesus Christ his Son cleanseth us from all sin." (1 John 1:7)

Cleansing is dependent upon our willingness to walk in the light, heeding God's Word, doing His Will, obeying His precepts!

Some wrongfully suppose this is a teaching of works for salvation. We would reply that while it is true we are saved by grace through faith and not of works, yet when our Lord returns, He will reward every man according to his works. (Revelation 22:12)

It is very much apparent that as we come to the close of this age that faith will be anemic and shallow so that God has no alternative but to allow a time of testing to come to professing Laodicean believers who are unprepared for rapture. For all such believers, the Lord's Return is not a comforting hope.

As D. M. Panton, British biblical scholar writes: "Too many are assuming that preparation for Christ's Coming is solely a matter of past experience and not at all a matter of walk, so that for all the saved, no matter how un-Christlike a life they live, it will be pure, unmixed, inevitable joy — an instant, miraculous deliverance so wrapped up in the gift of salvation that it covers even the most unconsecrated, unholy child of God."

Observes Panton: "There is and can be, so long as this teaching is believed; no demand for sanctity beyond salvation, and the tremendous thunders of the fast-approaching tribulation leave myriads of Christians unawake. The issue is a grave one, for our Lord's outburst from heaven to catch His bride away is either a comforting opiate for disobedient disciples, or else it is one of the most rousing of all truths - IT CANNOT BE BOTH!"

While on one hand I do not want to rob anyone of the comfort of the "blessed hope," on the other hand, I would not want to leave anyone with a "false hope." If there is any reason for the need of this message it is because of admonitions warning us to be ready for our Lord's return. Furthermore, those who hold to the promise of the blessed hope and prepare for this event will be ready for our Lord's Coming. For He hath said, "He that hath this hope in Him purifieth himself, even as He is pure!" And again we read, "...his wife hath made herself ready!"

Enoch is a type of the translation saints. He was translated because he had a testimony that he pleased God. We're told the carnal mind is enmity against God. We might ask - Can we hope to please God as long as we have carnality in us?

God's will is that we forsake every known sin. We are even called upon to "lay aside every weight," that which would hinder us, hold us back, and keep us from being ready for rapture. Some things in our lives we may not call sin are nevertheless "weights" and may keep us from being ready for our Lord's coming.

Dr. R. A. Torrey, an associate of Moody, once asked: "What constitutes readiness for the coming of the Lord?" His reply: "Separation from the world's indulgence of the flesh, from the world's immersion in the affairs of this life, and intense daily earnestness in prayer." This, declared Torrey, "is the first part of preparation for the Lord's return."

There are other requirements if we would be ready for the rapture. We are to look for His soon appearing. We read, "...unto them that look for him shall he appear the second time without sin unto salvation." (Hebrews 9:28)

As W. Graham Scroggie writes: "Am I looking for the Coming of the Lord Jesus Christ?" His reply: "He began His gracious work in you and in me at the cross when He redeemed us, saved with a great salvation. He has been continuing His work in our spirits ever since that glad hour, unless we have hindered Him, but He is going to perfect His work. If our souls were saved at Calvary, and if our spirits are being saved through life, He is going to save our bodies, to give us a new medium of expression."

What a glorious hope is the "blessed hope." Remember, if we really want to be ready for our Lord's coming, WE CAN BE READY. "Faithful is He that calleth you who also will do it!" (1 Thessalonians 5:24)

The day of Christ's Coming is imminent but uncertain. Would the Scriptures urge us to "look" and to "wait" for our Lord's coming if the Church must needs go through the tribulation? Studies from the Greek text teach that Christ's coming is imminent, and that only the date is uncertain.

THE IMMINENCE OF CHRIST'S RETURN

It would seem to me that to expect the tribulation rather than rapture, and anticipate Antichrist rather than Christ, takes away the glorious aspect of the blessed hope and destroys the Scriptural teaching of the imminence of our Lord's return.

The Bible teaches that the day of Rapture is imminent but uncertain."No man knoweth the day nor the hour," said Jesus.

Lt. Col. Delcourt of the French Salvation Army said: "The Lord's return is imperative and imminent because of the terrible state of the world today!"

Indeed, signs all around us would reveal our Lord's coming to be near and hastening. There are continual wars and rumors of wars. Israel is returning to her land; and is paying for it with terror by extremists. Europe is uniting, and the world is as it was in the days of Lot and the days of Noah.

As one prophetic conference speaker related — it is not just a sign here and there, but a combination of major signs all happening at the same time that reveals our Lord's coming is imminent.

Arthur Petrie, writing in PROPHECY MONTHLY, calls attention to 1 Thessalonians 1:10 where we have the words: "And to wait for His Son from heaven." The word used here for "wait," he notes, is a present infinitive, and means to be constantly waiting for a person who went away, to come again.

Another verse stressing the imminence of our Lord's coming is found in Philippians 3:20: "For our conversation (citizenship) is in heaven: from whence also we LOOK for the Saviour, the Lord Jesus Christ." Notice, the Greek word for "look" is in the present tense, and might be rendered, we are always and constantly expecting the Saviour, our Lord Jesus Christ. H.A.W. Meyer, New Testament Greek scholar, says:"This word denotes the patient. attentive waiting which never slacks until realized."

Professor A.T. Robertson, another noted Greek scholar, says of this word "look" which is the Greek word,

APEKDECHOMETHA…"The picture is like that of a wife who watches at evening for her husband, who tarries. She steps out of the door, down the steps, finally out of the gate and looks away down the street with longing for his coming."

The idea of imminent waiting for our Lord's return is likewise expressed in such verses as 1 Corinthians 1:7 where we read, "That ye come behind in no gift; waiting for the coming of our Lord Jesus Christ." Also in Titus 2: 11-13 we read: "For the grace of God that bringeth salvation hath appeared to all men, Teaching us that denying ungodliness and worldly lusts, we should live soberly, righteously, and godly in this present world; LOOKING for that blessed hope, and the glorious appearing of the great God and our Saviour Jesus Christ."

According to these verses we are to be looking and waiting for our Lord's return. As the late author and publisher, Gordon Lindsay, wrote: "Now, there are some who say that preaching the imminency of Christ's second coming is wrong, that Christ cannot come now, and He will not come until after the Great Tribulation. This is a matter of tremendous importance.

"If no phase of the second coming of Christ can occur until after the reign of the Antichrist and the Great Tribulation, we must admit that the preaching of Christ's imminency is wrong. But this would make the words of Christ to become a puzzle: For He says, 'Watch ye therefore for ye know neither the day nor the hour wherein the Son of Man cometh.' (Matthew 25: 13)

"If Christ cannot come until after the tribulation, which lasts for three years and a half, then His coming is not imminent. We would not, then, be in hourly expectancy. .We should instead keep our eyes open for the rise of the Antichrist; then after he achieves power, we are to wait for three and a half years to elapse and then only could we expect the rapture to take place.

"Clearly if that is true, the major part of evangelical preaching on the second coming of Christ would have to be changed. The teaching of the imminency of His coming would be altogether erroneous."

Other quotes might be given stressing the imminency of our Lord's return. There is Archer Butler who said long ago, "It is His purpose thus to live in our faith and hope, remote yet near, pledged to no moment, possible at any; worshipped not with the consternation of the near, or the indifference of a distant certainty, but with the anxious vigilance that awaits a contingency ever at hand."

Also quoting Joseph Seiss who writes: "Ever, as the Church moves on through time, and above all in the days in which we live, the next thing for every Christian to be looking for in this world is the coming of Christ to fulfill what is written in this Book. The Bible tells of nothing between us and that day."

Yes, our Lord's coming is imminent. Only the day and hour are unknown.

Finally, we would give warning to those who no longer look for the rapture, but patiently prepare for the coming awful great tribulation. There is a danger of accepting the role of the servant in the parable who says in his heart, "My Lord delays His coming." (Matthew 24:48)

As Dr. M. R. DeHaan points out: "Nowhere in all the Scriptures do we find a more solemn judgment pronounced than upon the servant who said in his heart: "My Lord delayeth His coming." Asks DeHaan: Just what is implied in "delaying our Lord's return?" Simply stated, he notes, "It is to deny the imminency, that is. the 'any moment' return of the Lord Jesus Christ."

Notes DeHaan: "There is not one verse in the entire Bible

which tells us to look, wait, watch, or prepare for any single event other than the' coming of the Lord Jesus Christ."

Thus, we, too, encourage all to be constantly looking for our Lord's coming, and to so live as to be ready. For He hath said, "Be ye therefore ready also for in such an hour as ye think not, the Son of man cometh."

CHAPTER 6
ADMONITIONS IN VIEW OF CHRIST'S RETURN

Perhaps you are like many who ask: What does it mean to be ready for Christ's return? Knowing that we have decided for Jesus Christ—isn't this enough to be ready for His coming? We might give the following suggestions from the Bible as to how believers can be ready for the rapture, when Jesus comes for His own.

1. PRAY ALWAYS!

"Watch ye therefore, and pray always, that ye may be accounted worthy to escape all these things that shall come to pass, and to stand before the Son of man." Luke 21:36.

R. A. Torrey comments: "According to this passage there is only one way in which we can be prepared for the coming of the Lord when He appears; that is, through much prayer." Notes Dr. Torrey: "The man who spends little time in prayer, who is not steadfast and constant in prayer, will not be ready for the Lord when He comes. But we may be ready. How? Pray! Pray! Pray!"

Keith Brooks says: "It would be hard to find any passage in the New Testament containing stronger words than found in the original of Luke 21:36, our Lord's warning to HIS OWN concerning the last days. Pray always is a word meaning the most urgent form of supplication and this all the time."

Chris Gerig comments in the GOSPEL HERALD that "Prayer demands the exercise of all our highest powers—hence the need of sobriety and vigilance Prayer will arm the soul for the events of the future. It will make strong for any emergency the believer may have to face. It will keep us in spiritual condition to be of some practical help and blessing to the souls which we contact from day to day. Prayer will keep us ready for the Lord's coming."

2. WATCH

Jesus said: "Take ye heed, watch and pray: for ye know not when the time is. For the Son of man is as a man taking a far journey, who left his house, and gave authority to his servants, and to every man his work, and commanded the porter to watch.

"WATCH ye therefore: for ye know not when the master of the house cometh, at even, or at midnight, or at the cock-crowing, or in the morning; lest coming suddenly he find you sleeping. And what I say unto you I say unto all, Watch." Mark 13:33-37.

If by being saved we are automatically ready for Christ's coming, then why all of these urgent commands to watch? In fact, four different times of the day we are told to be on the alert.

Incidentally, the first time when you read, "Watch", it is the Greek word "agoupneite" meaning "Wake up." Later uses of the word "Watch" is the Greek word "gregoreite" which means, "Stay awake! Be on your guard!"

Bishop J. C. Ryle suggests the following: "Watch against the leaven of false doctrine. Watch against slothfulness about Bible study and private prayer; watch against bitterness and uncharitableness toward others. Watch against pride and self-conceit."

Vance Havner once said: "The church needs not only to wake up but to get up." John Wesley, in his journal, once expressed his concern that "Nine in ten of those once-awakened are now faster asleep than ever."

In view of the soon-coming tribulation, how we need to heed this message to WATCH!

3. BE SOBER!

In view of the soon-coming of Christ, Paul admonishes: "Let us watch and be sober!" (1 Thessalonians 5:6-8)

Likewise, the Apostle Peter warns: "But the end of all things is at hand; be ye therefore sober!" (I Peter 4:7)

We are not to go around with long faces. Surely, we should have the joy of the Lord in our hearts. However, the Scriptures caution against foolish talking, jesting and joking which are not convenient...and admonitions in the Bible are often found calling for sobriety.

Centuries ago, when Jesus walked this earth, a man named Publius Lentullus, President of Judea, wrote concerning our Saviour: "It cannot be remembered that any have seen Him laugh, but many have seen Him weep." We need to be sober in view of His soon coming which may find many of our friends and family left behind to endure the wrath of God poured out in the tribulation.

4. BE CAREFUL FOR NOTHING!

Could it be that Satan's most effective weapon to defeat the Christian is to get him bogged down in the cares of this life?

In Philippians 4:5-6 we read..."The Lord is at hand...Be careful for nothing."

In the parable of the Sower ...the seed that fell among the thorns represented those whose lives were choked with cares, and riches and pleasures. (Luke 8:14)

In referring to His return, our Lord warns: "Take heed to yourselves lest at any time your hearts be overcharged with cares of this life, and so that day come upon you unawares. For as a snare shall it come on all them that dwell on the face of the whole earth." Luke 21:34-35.

Common ordinary cares of raising a family, making money,

building a house...legitimate duties, may find us so occupied as to be neglectful of our prayer life, Bible study, witnessing, and church attendance.

Today, many are like Martha, in the Bible, "full of cares and troubled about many things." She was active on behalf of Christ—tidying up the house and preparing a meal for the Lord. Reminds me of those who are occupied with church suppers, rummage sales and the like. However, of Mary, whose time was spent at the feet of Jesus, our Lord had said, "She hath chosen that good part which shall not be taken away from her."

5. BE PATIENT!

For centuries, believers have waited for the coming of our Blessed Lord. The reason, perhaps, that our Lord still has not returned is that He is not willing that any should perish but that all should come to repentance.

The Apostle James likens our Lord to a husbandman who waiteth for the precious fruit of the earth, and hath long patience for it!

Likewise, we too are exhorted to BE PATIENT! "Be ye patient, therefore brethren, unto the coming of the Lord. Be ye also patient; stablish your hearts; for the coming of the Lord draweth nigh." James 5:7-8

Without question we believe some are suffering a form of tribulation now. This tribulation may take the form of bodily affliction, trials, accidents, loss of property, and loss of loved ones. Nevertheless, tribulation is often God's way of purifying our lives and purging us that we may bring forth fruit.

Would we not rather have tribulation now than to live carelessly in worldly pleasure to find ourselves left behind at Christ's coming to go through tribulation such as the world h as never seen nor ever shall see again?

"Ye have heard of the patience of Job," writes James. Job, who had the misfortune of losing his property, livestock, servants, and even his children, and suffered bodily affliction as well, did not lose patience! Said he: "I know that my Redeemer liveth, and that He shall stand at the latter day upon the earth." Until that day when Christ shall come, "Be patient."

6. BE LOVING!

"We hate Christians. Even the best of them must be regarded as our worst enemies. For they teach love to one's neighbor. What we want is HATE. For only as we know how to hate can we conquer the universe." So spoke Lounacharski, former Commissar of Education in the U.S.S.R.

"A new commandment I give unto you, That ye love one another; as I have loved you," said Jesus. This kind of love whereof Jesus spoke results not from education but from conversion. "The love of God is shed abroad in our hearts by the Holy Ghost."

This kind of love will free us from racial prejudice; it will reduce frictions of disunity and dissention in our churches; it will alleviate many of the misunderstandings in our homes; and will help solve the problems of our community.

In view of Christ's soon coming, the Apostle John writes: "And the Lord make you to increase and abound in love one toward another, and toward all men...to the end he may stablish your hearts unblameable in holiness before God, even our Father at the coming of our Lord Jesus Christ with all His saints." I Thessalonians 3:12-13.

7. READ AND HEED GOD'S WORD.

I John 1:7 says: "If we walk in the light, as he is in the light, we have fellowship one with another, and the blood of Jesus

Christ his Son cleanseth us from all sin."

We need to read God's Word to know of His will for our lives, and how we can be ready for Christ's coming. Then we need to heed its message. We should have everything right between us and God, and between us and our fellowmen.

Thus, walking in the light of God's Word can mean that we're "paid up, prayed up, and ready to go up."

Like those "ever-ready" batteries, we can be ever ready to meet our Lord.

8. CURB YOUR APPETITE.

These should be days of fasting instead of feasting. Our Lord reminds us of the day when the Son of man would be taken away, saying: "But the days will come, when the bridegroom shall be taken away from them, and then shall they fast in those days." Luke 5:35.

Fasting will break the habits of life and put our faith on edge, making us conscious of the needs of others, while helping us to keep our bodies under control.

9. WARN THOSE WHO ARE UNPREPARED.

Our Lord Himself warned us that the tribulation would be a time of great trouble such as the world had never seen, no, nor ever shall see again.

Ezekiel would remind us that if we fail to warn men their blood will be upon us. (Ezekiel 3:17-21; 33:3-9)

The Apostle Paul said: "I ceased not to warn everyone night and day with tears." (Acts 20:31)

How much more burdened we should be for the lost and those who are living carelessly, seeing the coming of the Lord so close at hand. There are more warnings against the judgments of the great tribulation than there are concerning eternal doom.

How important to heed these loving admonitions and to

be ready-"for in such an hour as ye think not, the Son of man cometh." We should be living every moment so that if our Lord were to appear we wouldn't be embarrassed or ashamed but ready for His appearing.

10. COMFORT THE LONELY AND BEREAVED, THE DISCOURAGED AND DOWN-HEARTED.

After relating the details of our Lord's return, the Apostle Paul adds a word of comfort. He relates: "For if we believe that Jesus died and rose again, even so them also which sleep in Jesus will God bring with him." So we should rejoice in the fact that when our Lord appears, we will be reunited with loved ones, those who have gone before.

Then the Apostle explains: "For the Lord Himself shall descend from heaven with a shout, with the voice of the archangel, and with the trump of God: and the dead in Christ shall rise first: Then we which are alive and remain shall be caught up together with them in the clouds, to meet the Lord in the air, and so shall we ever be with the Lord." (I Thessalonians 4: 14-17) This is one of the clearest passages in the Bible that explains just what will happen when Jesus comes.

Finally, we are told, "Wherefore comfort one another with these words." (verse 18) How wonderful for those who are afflicted, for when Jesus comes, there will be no more sickness, no more pain, no more sorrow or tears, no more suffering or heartache.

For those who are ready to meet the Lord, it will be all joy and bliss. Wherefore, comfort one another with these words.

11. OBEY GOD.

How important it is to heed this Scriptural admonition. Hebrews 5:9 says our Lord "became the author of eternal salvation unto all them that OBEY Him." And in II Thessalonians 1:8 we read that our Lord comes "in flaming fire, taking vengeance on them that know not God, and that OBEY NOT the Gospel of our Lord Jesus Christ."

Study these verses and they'll remind you of the importance of obedience. Even the Gospel is to be "obeyed" as well as believed. For faith without works is dead. We need to exhibit by our lives that we are Christians if we call ourselves Christians.

12. REMEMBER, GOD'S WRATH IS UPON THE DISOBEDIENT.

It is true that the believer is not appointed to wrath. As we read in the following verses: "We wait for His Son from heaven, whom he raised from the dead, even Jesus, which delivered us from the wrath to come. For God hath not appointed us to wrath, but to obtain salvation by our Lord Jesus Christ, who died for us, that whether we wake or sleep, we should live together with Him." (I Thessalonians 1:10; 5:9-10)

On the other hand, we believe to live in willful sin or open disobedience to the revealed will of God as found in His Word, places us in a dangerous position of being left behind when Jesus comes.

For instance, the Lord in speaking to believers says: "But fornication, and all uncleanness, or covetousness, let it not be once named among you, as becometh saints; neither filthiness, nor foolish talking, nor jesting which are not convenient...Let no man deceive you with vain words: for because of these things cometh the wrath of God upon the children of disobedience. Be not ye therefore partakers with them." (Ephesians 5:3,4,6,7)

Thus, while God's wrath is not appointed for believers, we see where His wrath cometh upon the children of disobedience. May we "flee the wrath to come!"

13. BE WARNED OF SINNING WILFULLY.

As Hebrews 10:26 reminds us: "For if we sin willfully after that we have the knowledge of the truth, there remaineth no more sacrifice for sin, but a certain fearful looking for of judgment."

You can't sin willfully and get away with it. Christ cannot go back and be a sacrifice once again for sin. Rather, unless you get the victory over sin through the help of the Holy Spirit you may suffer the judgment of God's chastening wrath for your sin.

Some wrongfully suppose that when you're saved, you are forgiven of sins of the past, present and future. Romans 3:25 however speaks of "the remission of sins that are past" so that after you are saved it is wrong to suppose you can sin willfully and not be chastened. The tribulation, we believe, will be chastening for Laodicean Christians. For does not our Lord say: As many as I love, I rebuke and chasten: be zealous therefore, and repent." Revelation 3:19.

14. ABIDE IN CHRIST

In 1 John 2:28 we read: "And now, little children, abide in him, that when he shall appear, we may have confidence, and not be ashamed before him at his coming."

Will we be ashamed when Jesus comes? Not if we abide in Him. What does it mean to abide in Him? John reminds us: "Whosoever abideth in him sinneth not." (I John 3:6)

Ah, hear me, Our Lord would remind us there is coming a day when many will say, "Lord, Lord," and they will relate all of their achievements - how they did many wonderful works in His name, even cast out devils. But our Lord is heard saying: "Depart from me, ye that sin...that work iniquity." (See Matthew 7:21-23)

How important to be found abiding in Christ. Indeed, if we are found walking in the light God sheds on our pathway, living for Christ, His blood ever cleanses us from all sin. Thus we are kept ever ready for our Lord's coming,

15. INVEST IN SOULS

There is much more that could be said as to how to be ready for our Lord's return, or how best to occupy until He comes.

We must not forget the need of investing in the Lord's work. In many places the work of the Lord suffers for a lack of funds. Believing our Lord's coming is very close at hand, we would be reminded of the parable in Matthew 25 where those who invested their talents were rewarded with other talents, and our Lord commended them, saying: "Well done, thou good and faithful servant, enter thou into the joy of thy Lord."

However, to the unfaithful servant of whom it was said he "hid his lord's money," (He was cast into the outer darkness of tribulation, I believe, where there shall be weeping and gnashing of teeth,) our Lord said: "Thou oughtest therefore to have put my money to the exchangers and then at my coming I should have received mine own with usury."

How sad for many in that day when our Lord comes back and finds us hoarding needlessly, storing up that which could be used for bringing the gospel to precious souls around the world who need to hear this message.

16. SANCTIFY YOURSELVES.

There is something the Lord asks us to do and that is to yield ourselves fully to God. (Romans 12: 1-2)

He has a perfect plan, a pleasing blueprint for us to follow. Of Jesus it was said, "Lo, I come to do thy will, O God!"

How wonderful to surrender wholly to the will of God. We read further: "By which will we are sanctified." (Hebrews 10:9)

Sanctification seems to be such a hard word to explain, but it simply means "surrender to all of the revealed will of God!"

As we give ourselves fully to God, then His Spirit comes to dwell in fullness within us. This is what it means to be filled (or controlled) by the Spirit.

If we will invite the Lord to take over as the master of our lives, He will sanctify us, set us apart for Himself, and keep us ready for His coming.

"And the very God of peace sanctify you wholly; and I pray God your whole spirit and soul and body be preserved blameless unto the coming of our Lord Jesus Christ."

And notice-"Faithful is he that calleth you, who also will do it." (I Thessalonians 5:23-24)

If you want to be sanctified, and made ready for His coming, He will do it.

17. PURIFY YOURSELVES.

John writes: "Beloved, now are we the sons of God, and it doth not yet appear what we shall be: But we know that when he shall appear, we shall be like him; for we shall see him as he is." And then we read: "And every man that hath this hope, in him purifieth himself, even as he is pure." I John 3:2-3

I am convinced that if you want to be ready for our Lord's return you can be ready. In Revelation, speaking of the bride of Christ, the true church, we read: "His wife hath made herself ready!" Revelation 19:7.

18. SEEK OUT THE FELLOWSHIP OF OTHER LIKE-MINDED CHRISTIANS.

Attend services where the Word of God is preached, and the second coming of Christ is emphasized. In Hebrews 10:25 we read: "Not forsaking the assembling of ourselves together, as the manner of some is; but exhorting one another: and so much the more as ye see the day approaching."

These are days when you can get good gospel programs on radio and television. But the Bible reminds us that we need the warm, meaningful association of fellow-Christians. More than ever before we need to show love one to the other. Be friendly, be courteous, smile! Exhibit the fruit of the Spirit...love, joy, peace, long suffering, gentleness, kindness:

19. SEEK THE GIFTS OF THE HOLY SPIRIT.

In I Corinthians 1: 7, we read: "So that ye come behind in no gift; waiting for the coming of our Lord Jesus Christ..."

Through the indwelling Holy Spirit we are given gifts which will enable us to walk worthy of our calling, and will help us to be ready for Christ's coming. Not only are we told about these gifts, but encouraged to "covet earnestly the best gifts." I Corinthians 12:31.

20. BE READY.

"Be ye therefore ready!" Matthew 24:44. The Scriptures indicate that if you want to be ready, you can be ready. God looks upon your heart. And He knows if you will allow the Holy Spirit to occupy the throne of your life He will allow Jesus to be so real and precious that you'll want to live constantly in view of His coming.

As one writer declares: "The matter of being ready is of such supreme importance that our Lord has not left us without kindly admonition; and as willingness to serve naturally leads to preparedness for service, how vitally important it is that we consider what He has to say about being ready."

So, may we accept the verdict of God's Word and "Be ye therefore ready also, for in such an hour as ye think not, the Son of man cometh."

CHAPTER 7
WILL THE CHURCH GO THROUGH THE TRIBULATION?

Bible evangelicals are largely divided over one of the most-asked questions of our time— Will the Church go through the Tribulation? Believing our Lord's return is near and hastening, we would like to present a Bible-based answer to this all-important question.

There is a growing number of Christians who no longer believe the event we call the rapture is imminent, believing instead, that the Church will have to go through the Tribulation.

Fred John Meldau, writing in CHRISTIAN VICTORY magazine, notes: "There is an ever-growing controversy on whether the Church will be raptured before, in the midst of, or at the end of the Great Tribulation."

Perhaps several definitions are in order.

First, most all are in agreement that the Great Tribulation is a time of intense suffering and agony for the whole world. Our Lord says: "Then shall be great tribulation, such as was not since the beginning of the world to this time, no, nor ever shall be!"

As Dr. Charles J. Woodbridge writes concerning the Great Tribulation, he refers to it as "a specific era of anguish still in the future—a period of intense, excruciating sorrow and physical pain."

The question puzzling many is - Will Christ come before this Great Tribulation to rapture the saints? Or, is His coming confined only to the end of this period when He returns to establish His Kingdom?

TWO ASPECTS OF HIS COMING

Our Lord is coming again is a scriptural certainty believed by most Church leaders throughout history. John Knox, fiery Scottish preacher once shouted: "Shall our Lord not return?" He answered his own question by declaring: "We know that He shall return!" The return of our Lord is mentioned 318 times in the Bible. But what some fail to see is the two aspects of His second coming.

This is clearly brought out in 2 Timothy 4:1 which refers to our Lord's "appearing" and His "kingdom". We read how our Lord shall "judge the quick and the dead at His appearing and His kingdom." As the quick and the dead are two different groups of people to be judged at Christ's coming, so His appearing and His kingdom are two different times of His coming.

I'm reminded of traveling through the country one day when I came across a sign up ahead which said "FOR SALE". I supposed the property was for sale. Then, as I got closer, I could see there were more words on the sign and I detected the word "fish." So, I thought the sign must be saying: "FOR SALE FISH!" I wondered, who would be selling fish out here in the country. The thought was foolish and absurd. By that time, I came upon the sign to notice that it actually read: "FOR SALE FISH WORMS!"

This is how some people read the Bible. They know it speaks of our Lord's second coming, but they fail to see the two aspects of His coming. These two aspects are referred to in 2 Thessalonians 2:1, where reference is made to "the coming of our Lord Jesus Christ and our gathering together unto him."

When our Lord comes, He is seen establishing His kingdom as we pray, "Thy kingdom come!" Whereas, at our Lord's appearing, in the event we call the rapture, we are gathered together unto Him.

Even Malachi in the Old Testament speaks of "his coming" and "his appearing" relating these events to a time of purging and purifying. This helps to explain the purpose of the tribulation and the involvement of the Church. For writes Malachi: "Who may abide the day of his coming? and who shall stand when he appeareth? for he is like a refiner's fire and like fuller's soap!"

A refiner's fire and fuller's soap speaks of the cleansing and purifying that must come to a complacent, indifferent, lukewarm, Laodicean Church as we approach the end of this age.

For Malachi goes on to declare: "He shall sit as a refiner and purifier of silver." In Scripture, SILVER speaks of redemption. So our Lord is seen purifying those whom He has redeemed. It is true that the tribulation is a "time of Jacob's trouble" when God's purpose is to purge Israel. Malachi also mentions this, saying: "He shall purify the sons of Levi, and purge them as gold and silver, that they may offer unto the Lord an offering in righteousness." Malachi 3:3.

However, we must not overlook the fact that this age is going to end in a time of tribulation which will be for many a testing time. We repeat - God is left no choice but to allow many to be tested, as Peter declares: "The trial of your faith, being much more precious than of gold that perisheth, though it be tried with fire, might be found unto praise and honour and glory at the appearing of Jesus Christ." 1 Peter 1:7. Notice, Peter links this trial of faith to the appearing of Jesus Christ.

Now, the question many would ask is, "Will the Church go through this time of testing—this period of trial?"

It depends on which church you're in! We don't mean Baptist, Methodist or Presbyterian. Rather, the Scriptures would indicate that we are in either the Philadelphia Church or the Laodicean Church. The Philadelphia Church represents those who are truly born again and living for Christ, momentarily expecting our Lord's coming. These are wise virgins who have oil in their vessels with their lamps who, when the Bridegroom comes, go in to the marriage and the door is shut. For, concerning these Philadelphia believers, we read: "Because thou hast kept the word of my patience, I also will keep thee from the hour of temptation, which shall come upon all the world, to try them that dwell upon the earth." (Revelation 3:10)

Notice four things concerning these believers.

First, they not only "heard" the word – they "kept" it. Obedience is a requirement for being in this Philadelphia Church. It is also an evidence of our eternal salvation. As we read in Hebrews 5:9, we're reminded that Christ is the "author of eternal salvation unto all them that OBEY him."

In the second place, concerning the Philadelphia Church, we are told they will be KEPT from the hour of testing seen coming upon the whole world, to try them that dwell upon the earth.

Dr. T. J. McCrossan, noted Greek author, comments: "This Philadelphia church will be here right up to the very moment this great trial or tribulation, which is to cover the whole inhabited earth, is about to begin. We know this because Revelation 3:10 literally reads, "I also will keep thee (the Philadelphia Church) from, or away from, the hour or time (ek tes horas) of the trial, being about to come upon the whole inhabited earth to test or try them dwelling upon the earth."

What a blessed hope to be spared (kept) from this coming awful great tribulation.

In the third place, note that this coming tribulation will befall the whole world. Some think the tribulation is only for Israel, but as we read in Romans 2:9, "Tribulation and anguish, upon every soul of man that doeth evil, of the Jew first, and also of the Gentile." Notice, the tribulation spoken of here is not only for both Jew and Gentile, but for evil doers. For that reason alone the true Church is not seen undergoing tribulation of the Endtime. Yes, "in the world ye shall have tribulation." said Jesus. (John 16:33).

Trials, testing, suffering and pain are the lot of humanity including believers. As Paul declared, "We must through much tribulation enter into the kingdom of God." (Acts 14:22) Many are undergoing tribulation today in countries such as Russia and Red China. But concerning this Endtime Great Tribulation, we see where the promise to "keep out from" is given those in the Philadelphia Church who are then warned: "Behold, I come quickly: hold that fast which thou hast, that no man take thy crown." (Revelation 3: 11)

Finally, we believe it to be important again to stress that this tribulation is said to be for the purpose of TESTING and TRYING, although the Philadelphia Church will; be kept from this hour of temptation.

In 2 Peter 2:9, we read: "The Lord knoweth how to deliver the godly out of temptation..." The word for "temptation" used here is the same one used in Revelation 3:10, for the tribulation period. It is the Greek word PEIRASMOS, meaning "testing" or "trial." Thus, it is from this time of testing that the Philadelphia Church will be spared.

On the other hand, Dr. McCrossan gives four reasons why the Laodicean Church will go through this awful time of Great Tribulation.

First, because the Lord says: "I will spue thee out of my mouth!"

The second reason for believing the Laodiceans go through the tribulation is because there are those who are void of Christ's righteousness. These Laodiceans are counseled to "buy of Christ white raiment" that they may be clothed. The "white raiment" notes McCrossan, "is the righteousness of saints mentioned in Revelation 19:8, the only raiment that will assure us a place at the wedding supper."

The third reason why we believe the Laodicean Church will go through the Great Tribulation is because Christ made no provision to have it escape just before the tribulation comes to pass, as in the case of the Philadelphia Church.

Finally, this church goes through the tribulation because the very name "Laodicean" means "the people rule!" Says McCrossan: "In this church the people will assert their rights, and refuse to have their lives and conduct regulated by Christ and His Word." Notice, too, the outstanding characteristic of this church is its "lukewarmness." And it is to this church our Lord says, "As many as I love, I rebuke and chasten: be zealous, therefore, and repent!"

Amidst the chastening fires of earth's judgment there will come forth this great multitude of whom it is said: "These are they which came out of great tribulation, and have washed their robes, and made them white in the blood of the Lamb." (Revelation 7:14)

God's will is that we come clean now, that we repent from sin now, in order that we may be ready for Christ's coming. Or else, there is the danger of being left behind to go through this time of physical suffering and mental anguish seen coming upon the whole world. Today we hear a lot about "believe, believe, believe."

And, believe we must! But it is evident from the Scriptures that God doesn't accept our faith unless it is conditioned upon our repentance. We must turn from sin if we are to be genuinely converted.

There are some who will tell you the Laodiceans are only professing believers, that there are no true believers among them or they would not be spued out.

However, our Lord says, "As many as I love, I rebuke and chasten; be zealous therefore and repent."

Proof that there are believers among these Laodiceans is

evident from Hebrews 12:6, "For whom the Lord loveth He chasteneth, and scourgeth every son whom he receiveth."

Thus, the tribulation time will be for some, for the purpose of suffering, in order to be purified. As Peter declares: "He that hath suffered in the flesh hath CEASED FROM SIN." Suffering is one of God's ways to chasten His own. God punishes the wicked, but chastens His children, As we read, "For whom the Lord loveth he chasteneth, and scourgeth every son whom he receiveth. If ye endure chastening, God dealeth with you as with sons: for what son is he whom the father chasteneth not? But if ye be without chastisement, whereof all are partakers, then are ye bastards, and not sons!" (Hebrews 12:6-8)

The result of this chastening is that we might be "partakers of His holiness." Hebrews 12:10.

God's purpose is to present unto Himself a sanctified people. So in this same passage we're reminded to "Follow peace with all men, and holiness, without which no man shall see the Lord." Hebrews 12:15.

We read in Ephesians where God's purpose is to present to Himself, "a glorious church, not having spot, or wrinkle, or any such thing; but that it should be holy and without blemish." Ephesians 5:27.

Are we a part of this Church?

As to the question - Will the Church go through the tribulation, we repeat—it all depends what church you're in Laodicean or Philadelphian?

May the Lord lead us to see that if we are in the true Church, we will be looking for our Lord's appearing, and not for the tribulation. Furthermore, we will get ready for this all-glorious event. As John declares: "Every man that hath this hope in him purifieth himself, even as he is pure!"

Many scriptures suggest to us that our Lord is soon to come "for His saints" and then after the tribulation He will return to the earth "with His saints." His coming for His saints we call the RAPTURE or APPEARING.

His coming with His saints to judge the world and set up His kingdom is in reality His second coming. That there are these two aspects of our Lord's return, is suggested by such scriptures as Luke 17:22 and 26 where reference is made to the "days of the Son of man," and 1 Timothy 6:14-15 where at our Lord's return "in his times he shall show who is the blessed and only Potentate, the King of kings, and Lord of lords."

Scriptures which more clearly define this division might be cited as follows:

a. 2 Timothy 4:1 speaks of "his appearing and his kingdom."

b. 2 Thessalonians 2:1 mentions "the coming of our Lord Jesus Christ and our gathering together unto him."

c. Malachi 3:2 refers to "his coming" and "his appearing."

d. Luke 12:38 where our Lord's coming may occur in the "second watch" or "third watch".

RAPTURE... compared with SECOND COMING

1. RAPTURE:
   Referred to as the "day of Christ" (1 Corinthians 1:8)
   SECOND COMING:
   Spoken of as the "day of the Lord." (2 Peter 3:10)

2. RAPTURE:
   A time of Rewards. (2 Tim. 4:8; 1 Peter 5:4)
   SECOND COMING:
   A time of judgment for the ungodly. (2 Thess. 1:7-9)

3. RAPTURE:
   Our Lord comes for His saints. (1 Thess. 4:16-17)
   SECOND COMING:
   Our Lord returns with His saints.
   (Rev. 19:11-14; Jude 14; 1 Thess. 3:13; Zech. 14:5)

4. RAPTURE:
   Our Lord appears in the heavens as saints rise to meet Him. (1 Thess. 4:17)

SECOND COMING: Our Lord comes to the earth, judges the nations, and establishes His kingdom. (Zech.14)

5. RAPTURE: Those who are ready will accompany our Lord "to the marriage". (Mattew 25:10)
   SECOND COMING: Others will be ready only when our Lord returns "from the wedding." (Luke 12:36)

6. RAPTURE: This event is believed to occur "in a moment," hidden to earth's inhabitants. (1 Cor.15:52)
   SECOND COMING: Whereas, at our Lord's coming "every eye shall see him." (Revelation 1:7)

7. RAPTURE: The thought of His appearing brings comfort to the saints. (1 Thess. 4:18)
   SECOND COMING: Thoughts of the Day of the Lord produce fear. (Amos 5: 18; Mal.4:5; 1 Thess. 5:2)

More and more ministers, many of these noted evangelical leaders, are expressing belief that the Church will go through the tribulation. One minister offered $10,000 as a reward for anyone who could show from the Scriptures proof for the "pre-tribulation" theory.

Another offer of $500,000 in valuable property was made to a nationally-known radio broadcaster if he could furnish evidence that Christ will come for His own before the awful Great Tribulation.

Among those who believe that the Church will go through the tribulation is Dr. Oswald J. Smith, well-known missionary statesman and evangelical leader, who writes: "Now, after years of study and prayer I am absolutely convinced that there will be no rapture before the tribulation, but that the Church will undoubtedly be called upon to face the Antichrist, and that Christ will come at the close and not at the beginning of that awful period." He has since changed his beliefs.

Dr. Smith speaks of the influence of other writers on the

subject, including that of Augustine who declared: "The kingdom of Antichrist shall fiercely, though for a short time, assail the Church."

H. A. Baker wrote: "For eighteen centuries the fundamental principle of tribulation to glory was the universal belief of the truly born-again members of the Church."

However, Harnak, the great patriotic scholar, taught quite the opposite, suggesting that in the apostolic churches the idea of EXPECTATION was "inseparable from the Gospel!"

It is pointed out by some that a great number of Bible scholars and noted Christian leaders reject the idea of an imminent rapture. Among the names given are: A. J. Gordon, Dr. Carl F. Henry, Dr. Harold J. Ockenga, G. Campbell Morgan, Bishop Frank Houghton, Dr. A. B. Simpson, Dr. Horatius Bonar, George Mueller, Charles Spurgeon, and Hudson Taylor.

It is also indicated that in 1831 a certain woman claimed revelation that the true Church would be caught up to heaven before the tribulation.

It is further claimed that John Darby, active among the Plymouth Brethren, influenced many including C. I. Scofield, who made the view popular in the Scofield Bible.

I want to give you three major Scripture portions which some say indicate our Lord will not return until AFTER the tribulation.

First, there is our Lord's teaching in Matthew 24:29-31 which states: "Immediately after the tribulation of those days shall the sun be darkened, and the moon shall not give her light, and the stars shall fall from heaven, and the powers of heaven shall be shaken: and then shall appear the sign of the Son of man in heaven: and then shall all the tribes of the earth mourn, and they shall see the Son of man coming in the clouds of heaven with power and great glory. And he shall send his angels with a great sound of a trumpet, and they shall gather together his elect from the four winds, from one end of heaven to the other."

I would point out, however, in verses 27-28, just preceding this passage, we read: "For as the lightning cometh out of the east, and shineth even unto the west: so shall also the coming of the son of man be. For wherever the carcass is, there will the eagles be gathered together."

So we ask - Could this not represent the swift action of our Lord's coming at the rapture? For like an eagle seizing its prey, so our Lord comes for His own. The word "carcass" is the Greek word, PTOMA, meaning "a body fallen in death," which could refer to the saints who will be resurrected at our Lord's coming.

It is erroneous to assume that all of these men believed the Church would go through the tribulation. Rather some believe in the select-rapture which will find all who were not ready for Christ's Coming facing tribulation judgment.

The second Scripture used by certain Bible teachers to refute the idea of a rapture before the tribulation is found in 1 Corinthians 15:51-52 where we read: "Behold I shew you a mystery: we shall not all sleep, but we shall all be changed, in a moment, in the twinkling of an eye, at the last trump..."

We must examine this Scripture closely as at one time I, myself, was almost convinced that these verses linked the rapture to the sounding of the "last trump" of Revelation. Now notice, this verse says we shall be changed "in a moment, in the twinkling of an eye, at the last trump..."

Could it be that this change takes place at both the time of rapture as well as at the revelation of Jesus Christ? Notice! When our Lord suddenly appears from heaven at the rapture, we shall arise to meet him "in a moment, in the twinkling of an eye!" Literally, in an atom of time, we shall receive our glorified bodies.

Then again this change will take place "at the last trump." Bible teachers who do not accept the rapture say the "last trump" refers to Revelation 11:15-18 where we have an angel sounding the seventh trumpet, an event which occurs at the end of the tribulation. For we read, "And the nations were angry, and thy wrath is come, and the time of the dead, that they should be judged, and that thou shouldst give reward unto thy servants the prophets, and to the saints, and them that fear thy name, small and great..."

According to this Scripture, the blowing of the seventh trumpet occurs following the period of wrath seen sweeping the earth. So this would contradict the Scripture which tells us, "God hath not appointed us to wrath!" (1 Thessalonians 5:9)

It is true that at the blowing of the seventh trumpet of Revelation there will be a time of resurrection and giving of rewards. And at this time the saints will be judged. But I believe there is a rapture that will occur before this final resurrection of saints that died during the tribulation period.

Finally; a third scripture used by those who do not believe in a rapture as occurring before the tribulation, is 2 Thessalonians 2:1-3. These verses tell us - "Now we beseech you, brethren, by the coming of our Lord Jesus Christ, and by our gathering together unto him, that ye be not soon shaken in mind, or be troubled, neither by spirit, nor by word, nor by letter as from us, as that the day of Christ is at hand. Let no man deceive you by any means: for that day shall not come, except there come a falling away first, and that man of sin be revealed, the son of perdition."

We're told Antichrist must come first and then there will follow the coming of Christ. However, again I would point out that Paul here is referring to the "Day of the Lord."

Notice chapter one of 2 Thessalonians where Paul speaks

of the Lord being revealed from heaven with his mighty angels, in flaming fire. This is not the rapture, but the revelation! So, in this second chapter, Paul is saying this "Day of the Lord" will not come until Antichrist first appears. Thus, Antichrist's appearance is followed by the Revelation of Christ when He returns in flaming fire to take vengeance on them that know not God and that obey not the gospel of our Lord Jesus Christ!

This appearance of Christ is to bring wrath on the ungodly, and not to catch away a bride. Again, I cannot accept the belief of some that this passage relates to the rapture. Rather, it refers to the revelation when He shall be revealed from heaven in flaming fire to punish the wicked. Thus, Paul goes on to assure us not to be troubled or shaken in mind concerning the coming of Christ and our gathering together unto Him, which event I believe to be the rapture.

These are rather difficult verses to explain. Unless you have your Bibles open and following, it is not always clear to present these wonderful truths. Be assured, however, the important thing is to be ready whenever our Lord does come. For He hath said, "Be ye therefore ready also, for in such an hour as ye think not the Son of man cometh."

CHAPTER 8
PRE-TRIBULATION RAPTURE... A NEW BELIEF?

A letter that has come to my desk asserts that the Pre-tribulation theory of the coming of Christ did not begin until 1830. Furthermore, this letter claims to have offered property valued at $500,000 if this theory could be proved from the Bible.

The late Dr. John Walvoord, former president of Dallas Theological Seminary wrote: "In the early Church there was daily expectation continued among the early Church fathers." (Moody Monthly, January, 1955)

Exhortations to "wait" and "look" cannot be explained if great tribulation comes first, notes Walvoord. While we recognize there were those who also held the position that certain definite signs must be fulfilled before Christ would appear, there was the constant reminder that Christ's Return was ever imminent although no man knew the day nor the hour.

Examples we might cite include Hermas, believed to have been mentioned by the Apostle Paul in Romans 16:14. In a vision Hermas was told: "You have escaped from the great tribulation on account of your faith, and because you did not doubt in the presence of the beast Go, therefore, and tell the elect of the Lord His mighty deeds, and say to them that this beast is a type of the great tribulation that is coming. If ye, then, prepare yourselves, and repent with all your heart, and turn to the Lord, it will be possible for you to escape it, if your heart be pure and spotless, and ye spend the rest of your lives serving the Lord blamelessly." (from The Shepherd of Hermas, about 100-120 A.D.)

Here, then, is evidence of one closely associated with the Apostle Paul who verifies the fact of belief in the possibility of escape from coming tribulation of those who were faithful in making preparation for our Lord's Return.

Other quotations include:

Cyprian, Bishop of Carthage (220-250 A.D.) "Let us ever in anxiety and cautiousness be waiting the second coming of the Lord..."

Clement of Rome (about 95 A.D.) and undoubtedly a fellow-laborer with Paul, wrote in his Second Epistle, "If therefore we shall do what is just in the sight of God, we shall enter into His kingdom, and shall receive the promises which neither eye hath seen, nor ear heard, nor have entered into the heart of man. Wherefore, let us every hour expect the kingdom of God in love and righteousness, because we know not the day of the Lord's appearing."

An outstanding quotation comes from the Didache, a treatise of the early Second Century in which the urgency of readiness was stressed. We quote: "Watch for your life's sake: let your lamps be not quenched and your loins be not ungirded, but be ye ready, for you know not the hour in which your Lord cometh!"

This seems to be the only safe, scriptural position.

Archbishop Trench similarly spoke of the daily expectation of Christ's coming as "possible any day, impossible no day."

Martin Luther declared:"Christ designed that the day of His coming should be hid from us, that being in suspense, we might be as it were upon the watch."

D. M. Panton, noted British scholar, writes: "God has not revealed the date of the second coming of Christ, in order that we may always be watchful; nor has He revealed the standard of holiness for rapture, in order that we may be always pressing on to perfection."

It is said of the saintly Horatius Bonar, his last act before turning to his pillow upon retiring was to look up to the heavens and whisper, "Perhaps tonight, Lord?" In the morning, his first movement was to greet the day with the appeal, "Perhaps today, Lord?"

But is this not the scriptural way? Should we not be concerned that we might be ready at any hour of the day our Lord might come?

In Mark's gospel we have this parable. Read it carefully:

"For the Son of man is as a man taking a far journey, who left his house, and gave authority to his servants, and to every man his work, and commanded the porter to watch. Watch ye, therefore: for ye know not when the master of the house cometh, at even, or at midnight, or at the cockcrowing, or in the morning: Lest coming suddenly he find you sleeping. And what I say unto you I say unto all, Watch!" (Mark 13:34-37)

Here mentioned are four times of the day our Lord may return. And in view of His unannounced coming we are commanded to Watch! For our Lord reminds us this message is not only for His disciples only but for all.

Previously our Lord had related the parable of the fig tree. This we believe symbolizes the return of Jews to Palestine and the restoration of Israel as a nation. It is in view of this event that our Lord's coming is said to be at the "doors" (plural) referring to both His appearing and glorious return.

It is also in view of Israel's revival as a nation that we are reminded "this generation shall not pass, till all these things be done!" In other words, it is generally believed that those on earth who see Israel back in her land will witness the consummation of all things which includes the return of Christ back to this earth.

Then we read, "But of that day and that hour knoweth no man, no, not the angels which are in heaven, neither the Son, but the Father. Take ye heed, watch and pray: for ye know not when the time is."

Of this we believe we can be certain. Witnessing Israel's restoration to her land, we believe we can expect our Lord's Return to be near and hastening. In Psalms 102:16 we read, "When the Lord shall build up Zion He shall return in his glory."

While some may argue that Israel's return is in unbelief, nevertheless, the evidence would substantiate God's dealings in preserving and protecting against all odds. Surely God's miraculous leadership is very much in evidence. Israel is back in her land, and nations within Europe are fast forming the revived Roman Empire as evidenced in the many nations who are now a part of the European Union. Eventually we can expect one called Antichrist who will head this economic-political federation who will make a covenant with Israel as predicted in Daniel 9:27.

Witnessing these endtime events we are commanded to "Watch!" Two Greek words are used by Jesus. After relating the parable of the fig tree, He declared, "Take ye heed, Watch and pray; for ye know not when the time is!" The word "watch" is the Greek word "agoupneite" which means, "Stay awake! Remain alert! Be on your guard!"

As one noted conference speaker emphasized, "One of the main jobs of the Church today is not only to get Christians awake, but to get them out of bed." So, "Be ye ready also, for in such an hour as ye think not, the Son of man cometh!"

CHAPTER 9

ELEVEN REASONS WHY WE BELIEVE MANY WILL MISS THE RAPTURE!

In North Hollywood, California, the 2000-member First Assembly of God church has gone on record as changing the church by-laws to allow for the continued operation of the ministry following the event we call the Rapture.

Noted Dr. D. Leroy Sanders, the congregation's pastor:"The blessed hope clearly speaks of an instantaneous and general translation of the Assembly members. All pastors, deacons, elders, and other leaders and officers are expected to be caught up alive in a moment of time, thus depriving the church of duly constituted legal representation."

The church ruled that in the event of the rapture having taken place, "the remaining members...shall meet in an emergency church council the following Sunday morning at 11 o'clock and elect...a temporary chairman." Dr. Sanders said the chairman would be empowered to call for a new church council to oversee operations of the 1.5 million dollar property.

Some think it preposterous that there should be a rapture of the Church, while others who believe in the event of the Rapture see every professing believer "caught up" at the return of Christ. What does the Scripture say?

The Bible does teach that there's a day coming when "the Lord himself shall descend from heaven with a shout, with the voice of the archangel, and with the trump of God: and the dead in Christ shall rise first: Then we which are alive and remain shall be caught up together with them in the clouds, to meet the Lord in the air: and so shall we ever be with the Lord." (I Thessalonians 4:16-17)

This is the event many Bible evangelicals call the Rapture. Today we would like to list ten reasons why we believe there will be those looking for the Rapture who will miss this event, and hence will remain behind to go through the tragic period known as the Great Tribulation.

Scriptural admonitions warn of those whose salvation is not questioned, but because of unfaithfulness, worldliness, spiritual lukewarmness, immorality...they are unprepared to meet the Lord. So they are left behind at the Rapture to pass through the trying period of awful affliction, to come through this fiery trial "purged and purified."

While some agree that "willful sin" must be punished by "fiery indignation" (Hebrews 10:26-27), and that "chastening" follows disobedience (Hebrews 12:6-8), they are not willing to concede that the tribulation may be that form of chastening that befalls a lukewarm Church at the coming of Christ. Yet, the Scripture clearly teaches concerning the Laodiceans of our church age, that they will be spewed out if neither hot nor cold. And they will be chastened if they are Christ's own- "For whom the Lord loveth he chasteneth, and scourgeth every son whom he receiveth." (Hebrews 12:6)

Rapture truly is the reward of readiness, scripturally. The fact that many will miss this glorious event is taught as evidenced in the following Biblical passages.

1. Jesus taught that some who looked for His coming will miss it. He said, "The days will come when ye shall desire to see one of the days of the Son of man, and ye shall not see it." (Luke 17:22)

There are, in reality, two days of our Lord's Return referred to in 2 Timothy 4:1 as "his appearing" and "his kingdom." When our Lord appears the saints will be caught up to meet Him. And when our Lord returns to this earth, He comes to establish His millennial kingdom.The implication of Scripture would seem to be that some who anticipate the day of rapture will miss it.

2. Revelation 7:7-14 indicates that "a great multitude" will be left behind at the coming of Christ to go through the Great Tribulation. It is said of these tribulation saints that they "washed their robes, and made them white in the blood of the Lamb."

The evidence is that their robes were defiled, spotted and dirty at the coming of the Lord and amidst tribulation they repented, although many may have died for their faith.

On the basis of this Scripture, the late G. Campbell Morgan stated: "Personally, I am convinced that not all Christian people will be taken to be with Christ on His return, but only those who by the attitude of their lives are ready for His appearing."

3. The Parable of the Ten Virgins found only half of those looking for the coming bridegroom ready for His appearance. (Matthew 25:1-13)

Whatever interpretations are made of this parable, it is plainly shown that five were ready and went into the marriage at the coming of the Bridegroom while the remaining five missed the event.

Scofield writes: "That the marriage of the Lamb takes place in heaven is clear from Revelation 19:1 with verses 7-10 where we read in part, 'Blessed are they which are called unto the marriage supper of the Lamb.'"

Thus, there is special blessing to those who are raptured. As evidenced in Revelation 5:9-10, the raptured saints, we believe, represent those who are "kings and priests" unto God who will reign upon the earth, whereas those left behind to go through the tribulation are classified as "servants."

(Revelation 7:15). So, which would we sooner be—a servant or a king or priest? Should we not seek to make our calling and election sure?

Incidentally, the promise of reigning with Christ is for the overcomers. "To him that overcometh will I grant to sit with me in my throne." (Revelation 3:21) "But the Church has refused as a whole to overcome self, the world, and the devil," writes Sarah Foulkes Moore, editor of HERALD OF HIS COMING. "On the contrary," she notes, "The church is overcome by them. Hence her royal estate as the Bride of Christ is given to those who will overcome as individuals, and it is they who will inherit the promise given to overcomers, and will sit with Christ as His consort on His throne and rule with Him. Having ruled over the world, the flesh, and the devil in this life, they will be accounted worthy to sit with Him on His throne."

4. A parallel parable in Luke 12:35-40 would indicate some will not be ready until our Lord returns from the wedding. The Scripture reads as follows:

35… Let your loins be girded about, and your lights burning;

36… And ye yourselves like unto men that wait for their lord, when he will return from the wedding; that when he cometh and knocketh, they may open unto him immediately,

37… Blessed are those servants, whom the lord when he cometh shall find watching: verily I say unto you, that he shall gird himself, and make them to sit down to meat, and will come forth and Serve them.

38… And if he shall come in the second watch. or come in the third watch, and find them so, blessed are those servants.

39… And this know, that if the goodman of the house had known what hour the thief would come, he would have watched, and not have suffered his house to be broken through.

40… Be ye therefore ready also: for the Son of man cometh at an hour…

This passage in Luke 12:35-48, although seldom preached on, teaches that:

A. Some won't be ready until our Lord returns from the wedding. (Luke 12:35)

B. That the possibility exists that our Lord may come at two different times, described as the second watch or third watch. (Luke 12:38).

C. That if the one in charge would have watched the house had not been broken through. (Luke 12:39)

D. That the servant who looked for His Lord's coming but who lived carelessly shall be left behind with "unbelievers." (Luke 12:46)

E. That depending on the servant's knowledge of the Lord's will, he will be beaten with few stripes or many stripes.

Notice: It's apparent this judgment will be confined to earth, and specifically to the Great Tribulation. There are no beatings in heaven as far as can be seen, but a joyous reunion of fellowship and bliss in the presence of the Bridegroom.

5. The Apostle Paul spoke of the "resurrection from among the dead" as a prize to be gained, saying: "I press toward the mark (the goal) for the prize of the high calling (upward calling) of God in Christ Jesus." Philippians 3:14.

Again Sarah Foulkes Moore notes: "Many Christians today are taking for granted they are ready. How different is their slothful attitude from that of the great apostle, Paul.

At the time he was writing the Philippians (Philippians 3:10) he was not sure he had met the requirements of readiness for the first resurrection. He said, "Not as though I had already attained…but I press toward the mark." He lived his daily Christian experience as a man running a race with the purpose in view of winning a prize. The prize Paul desired to win was Christ, the Bridegroom. He already knew Christ as Lord and Saviour. Later he admitted to having attained that goal saying, "I have kept the faith: henceforth there is laid up for me a crown of righteousness which the Lord, the righteous Judge, shall give me at that day." 2 Timothy 4:7-8.

6. That "crowns" may be lost is stressed by John in Revelation 3:11, indicating the possibility of losing the reward of being raptured. We read: "Behold I come quickly, hold that fast which thou hast, that no man take thy crown."

While salvation is a gift, it is clearly taught that there are rewards to be gained in running the Christian life. While there is no evidence that the "rapture" is included in salvation, it behooves us to examine the Scriptures to see if it may be one of the "crowns" or "rewards" given to the faithful.

D. M. Panton writes: "Too many are assuming that preparation for Christ's coming is solely a matter of past experience and not at all a matter of walk, so that for all the saved, no matter how unChristlike a life they live, it will be pure, unmixed, inevitable joy—an instant, miraculous deliverance so wrapped up in the gift of salvation that it covers even the most unconsecrated child of God."

Declares Panton: "There is and can be, so long as this teaching is believed, no demand for sanctity beyond salvation, and the tremendous thunders of the fast-approaching tribulation leaves myriads of Christians unawake. The issue is a grave one, for our Lord's outburst from heaven to catch His bride away is either a comforting opiate for disobedient disciples, or else it is one of the most rousing of all truths — IT CANNOT BE BOTH."

7. The history of the Laodicean Church is that it would be "spewed out" at the coming of the Lord.

Some doubt that these Laodiceans were actual believers.

The Scriptures would indicate that they were true believers of a sort but that their faith was shallow, and their testimony was "lukewarm." And our Lord goes on to assert, "As many as I love, I rebuke and chasten; be zealous therefore, and repent."

The Tribulation is a time of chastening is clear for all to see. God does not chasten the wicked but punishes them. He chastens His own.

One writer expresses the belief shared by many that Christ's death on the cross atoned for sins of the past, present and future and regardless of the life we live we are automatically ready for His coming. Christ's shed blood is thus efficacious regardless of the life we may be found living at the time of rapture.

On the other hand, this author says I Corinthians 3:11-15 and I Corinthians 11:30-32 plainly teach that believers who may be disobedient are chastened in this life, but not lost even if they die in that state; however, they will lose their reward and be ashamed. This is exactly what I am trying to say. The Tribulation, I believe, will serve as chastening for disobedient disciples.

8. The history of the Philadelphia Church, on the other hand, gives promise to those who keep God's Word that they will also be kept from the "hour of temptation that shall come upon all the world, to try them that dwell upon the earth." Revelation 3: 10.

Peter writes: "The Lord knoweth how to deliver the godly out of temptation..." 2 Peter 2:4. The word "Temptation" used here is the same Greek word PEIRASMOS for "temptation" found in Revelation 3:10. That the godly will be spared this awful judgment seen coming upon the world is evident from this Scripture.

9. Promises concerning the Wrath of God would indicate

the possibility of escape from coming awful tribulation providing certain conditions are met.

IThessalonians 5:9 reminds us:"God hath not appointed us to wrath, but to obtain salvation by our Lord Jesus Christ, Who died for us, that, whether we wake or sleep, we should live together with him." On the other hand, we read:"The wrath of God is revealed from heaven against all ungodliness and unrighteousness…" Romans 1:19; (See also Romans 2:5-10)

And writing to the Ephesians the Apostle Paul warns of many corrupt practices concerning which many Christians — are guilty; such as fornication, uncleanness, covetousness, foolish talking—saying: "Let no man deceive you with vain words for because of these things cometh the wrath of God upon the children of disobedience." (Ephesians 5:6)

10. Several Old Testament passages collaborate the teaching that many will succumb to a period of trial that serves as a purging and purifying test that is linked to the endtime.

Daniel writes: "And some of them of understanding shall fall, to try them, and to purge, and to make them white, even to the TIME of the End" (Daniel 11:35)

"Many shall be purified, and made white, and tried; but the wicked shall do wickedly: and none of the wicked shall understand."

Malachi writes:"Who may abide the day of his coming? And who shall stand when he appeareth? For he is like a refiner's fire, and like fullers' soap. And he shall sit as a refiner and purifier of silver: and he shall purify the sons of Levi, and purge them as gold and silver, that they may offer unto the Lord an offering in righteousness." Malachi 3:2-3

Note: Regardless as to how you read these passages, they teach God's purpose to refine and purify through trial and affliction.

Did not our Lord speak of the coming great tribulation as a time of "affliction, such as was not from the beginning of the creation which God created unto this time, neither shall be." Mark 13:19. Peter writes of one of the purposes of affliction, saying: "He that hath suffered in the flesh hath ceased from sin." (I Peter 4:1)

One of God's purposes may be to allow tribulation and affliction to come to purify those who are not ready for entrance into His holy presence. For does our Lord not say, "Follow peace with all men, and holiness, without which no man shall see the Lord:" Hebrews 12:14.

Just as many of our Prisoners of War had their faith perfected as a result of tortures and imprisonment, so Peter would remind us of how it will be with believers, saying: "The trial of your faith, being much more precious than of gold that perisheth, though it be tried with fire, might be found unto praise and honour and glory at the appearing of Jesus Christ." (I Peter 1:7)

Notice, it is in view of our blessed hope of Christ's appearing that we are told: "And every man that hath this hope in him purifieth himself, even as he is pure." (I John 3:3)

We would ask— What if a believer who is living in known sin does not purify himself, does not come clean from filthy practices and unclean habits which the Scriptures condemn? Is there any choice but for God to allow the purifying judgment of the Great Tribulation to serve as a furnace of affliction upon the sinful and disobedient?

Thus, the Apostle John writes: "And now, little children, abide in him; that, when he shall appear, we may have confidence, and not be ashamed before him at his coming." (I John 2:28) The Apostle goes on to explain: "Whosoever abideth in him sinneth not." So to abide in Christ means to be ready by the attitude of our lives, not living in willful known sin, lest as the Greek rendering of this previous verse reads, "in shame we shrink back from him at his coming."

How many will not be ready for the coming of the Lord? Did not Jesus again remind us: "Many will say to me in that day, Lord, Lord, have we not prophesied in thy name? and in thy name have cast out devils? and in thy name done many wonderful works? And then will I profess unto them, I never knew you: depart from me, ye that work iniquity." (Matthew 7:21-23)

What a high standard of profession to be doing all that. Yet because of sin in the lives of those who performed these acts, and on account of iniquity our Lord says: "I never knew you." It is therefore obvious that we can believe, and yet if we never truly repent, our Lord doesn't know us, and does not accept our faith. For faith without works is dead.

11. Finally, (but not last) the evidence of many missing the rapture to go through the tribulation is illustrated in the flood. As Noah rode over the flood, so the raptured saints will be raised by being "caught up" into the presence of our wonderful Lord at His coming. And as many during the flood called upon the Lord, amid the choking, screaming cries of repentance, our Lord heard, and when He died He went to these spirits in their captivity and preached unto them.

Peter writes: "For Christ...went and preached unto the spirits in prison; which sometime were disobedient, when once the longsuffering of God waited in the days of Noah, while the ark was a preparing, wherein few, that is, eight souls were saved by water." (I Peter 3:19-20)

Why did our Lord preach to those who died in the flood? We read: "For this cause was the gospel preached also to them that are dead, that they might be judged according to men in the flesh, but live according to God in the spirit." (I Peter 4:6)

It is difficult for us to understand the workings of God's grace, as well as His chastenings. But concerning the Corinthian fornicator you'll recall Paul committed him "unto Satan for the destruction of the flesh, that the spirit may be saved in the day of the Lord Jesus Christ." (I Corinthians 5:5)

It is my conviction that the great tribulation will be God's judgment upon the disobedient, whose fate may be the destruction of their flesh by cruel tortures ending in death, although God's grace will permit their prayers to be heard as they cry unto him in the agony of repentance.

Think of what it would be like for Jesus to come today and you were left behind. Would you not search your heart to discover the reason why? And as God reveals in your own conscience the disobedience in following the fleshly lusts and worldly pursuits instead of living in holy anticipation for the heavenly bridegroom, would you not determine to die for your faith in Jesus Christ rather than surrender to the Antichrist? It will be terrible, for you cannot buy or sell unless you accept an identifying mark. Many will succumb to the temptation to satisfy their stomach's desire rather than starve to death.

On the other hand, a great multitude which no man can number will face the tribulation knowing they did not heed our message, "Be ye therefore ready." Like foolish virgins they chose to go on their merry way, ridiculing the message of "holy living" in view of Christ's coming, thinking all was right so long as they made a profession of faith in Christ.

What anguish! What disappointment! What unparalleled trouble ahead! What great awful tribulation which Jesus said was like no other period in the world's history-"not since the beginning of the world to this time, no, nor ever shall be." And he added, "Except those days should be shortened, there should no flesh be saved: but for the elect's sake those days shall be shortened."

While some think only the Jews are referred to here as the "elect" we are ever more convinced that many who looked for the rapture will miss this glorious event, and will constitute the elect of the endtime. The reference to "saints" in the tribulation is often mentioned in the book of the Revelation in reference to believers enduring the wrath of the Antichrist, and there is no other explanation than that many will miss the rapture.

Thus, we would conclude in the words of Jesus who warned us saying: "And take heed to yourselves, lest at any time your hearts be overcharged with surfeiting, and drunkenness, and cares of this life, and so that day come upon you unawares. For as a snare shall it come on all them that dwell on the face of the whole earth."

Our Lord warned, saying: "Watch ye therefore, and pray always, that ye may be accounted worthy to escape all these things that shall come to pass, and to stand before the Son of man." (Luke 21:34-36)

What does it mean to be "accounted worthy?"

Sarah Foulkes Moore observes: "It means the perfection of spiritual character attained in an overcoming life. It means devotion to the Person of the Lord Jesus Christ. It means a daily walk like that of Enoch who is a type of the translation saints and who had 'this testimony, that he pleased God.'"

May I ask you, are you praying to escape the coming great tribulation as Jesus warned? Or do you accept the idea that trusting Christ as Saviour automatically secures our position at the rapture?

Oh, may we heed the admonitions and warnings of God's Word that remind us "to make our calling and election sure." Not only are we called upon to heed the grace of God in salvation; but the grace of God also teaches us "that denying ungodliness and worldly lusts, we should live soberly, righteously, and godly, in this present world: Looking for that blessed hope, and the glorious appearing of the great God and our Saviour Jesus Christ; who gave himself for us, that he might redeem us from all iniquity, and purify unto himself a peculiar people, zealous of good works."

Do you think you can live as you please and excuse your sin as covered by the grace of God? This Scripture teaches otherwise. Rather, the grace of God calls us to holy living, and urges us to forsake worldly lusts for purity reflected in our behaviour and pattern of living. The church of Jesus Christ is the bride of our Lord and

Saviour. And God's purpose is to present to Himself "a glorious church, not having spot, or wrinkle, or any such thing; but that it should be holy and without blemish."

Are you a part of this Bride?

If so, God's message to you may be summed up as follows:

"Despise not prophesyings. Prove all things; hold fast that which is good. Abstain from all appearance of evil. And the very God of peace sanctify you wholly; and I pray God your whole spirit and soul and body be preserved blameless unto the coming of our Lord Jesus Christ."

What an assignment! Is it possible for God to preserve us blameless until His coming? The next verse reads: "Faithful is he that calleth you, who also will do it." (I Thessalonians 5:20-24)

Yes, I believe you can be ready if you want to be for our Lord's return. For our Lord hath said, "Be ye therefore ready also: for the Son of man cometh at an hour when ye think not." (Luke 12:40)

CHAPTER 10

POSSIBLE ERRORS CONCERNING THE RAPTURE

As many were mistaken concerning Christ's first coming, so we believe there will be many unprepared for His Return. Our Lord appeared as a lowly babe while he was expected to come as a reigning monarch. Christ was born in a stable, when it was expected He would be born in a palatial mansion.

It was expected that men would crown Him king. Instead, He was crucified. No, our Lord did not come as King but as Saviour, and was unrecognized by the vast majority of mankind, even though He came through the lineage of David and fulfilled all of the prophecies spoken of Him. Similarly, we can be sure our Lord's second coming will find many unprepared for events which surround the Rapture and His glorious return to earth.

For instance, here might be some of the errors surrounding His second coming:

ERROR No. 1...That all believers, regardless of carnality or sin in the life, will be raptured when Jesus comes.

Accordingly, if this is believed, then all of the admonitions and warnings given to believers to be ready for Christ's coming are unnecessary. What about those Scriptures urging us to be sober (I Peter 4:7); to watch and pray always (Luke 21:38); to be patient (James 5:7-8); to be faithful (Mattew 25:33); to be holy (Hebrews 12:14) and to be ready (Matthew 24:44) in view of our Lord's unannounced return?

Dr. V. Raymond Edman once said: "The imminent return of the Lord Jesus Christ is a powerful scriptural incentive to watchfulness and preparation for His return...a powerful incentive to holiness and consistency of life." Do you agree?

One well-known Bible teacher stated that when our Lord returns, He will rapture some from the theatre and the tavern. Of course, it is asserted that at the judgment seat of Christ all will be forgiven and the consequences may be a loss of rewards. I believe the Bible teaches that the Rapture may be a reward. It is the crown to those who love Christ's appearing. (2 Timothy 4:8)

To say our readiness depends to some degree on our own preparation is labeled by some as "works", whereas, we are saved by "grace."

While I admit it is by grace we are saved, yet I point out that when the Lord comes He will take our works into consideration. Listen to Revelation 22:12 where our Lord says: "Behold, I come quickly; and my reward is with me, to give every man according as his work shall be."

Then there are those who say that were the Lord to take some believers and leave the rest behind, it would rend the House of God—the Church. Yet, this is exactly what our Lord warned against, saying: "This know, that if the good man of the house had known what hour the thief would come, he would have watched, and not have suffered his house to be broken through. Be ye therefore ready also; for the Son of man cometh at an hour when ye think not." (Luke 12:39-40)

Again, the accusation is made that the "last generation" would be penalized if Christ at that time raptures only those who are ready. Actually, the last generation is the Laodicean Church age which finds many neither hot nor cold but "lukewarm. So our Lord is seen having no choice but to allow the chastening fires of tribulation to try the faith of those living at that time that they may come forth as gold. (I Peter 1:7)

It is said that for some believers to be left behind to go

through the tribulation would serve as a sort of purging time. With this idea the Scriptures agree, for in Daniel 11:35 we read: "And some of them of understanding shall fall, to try them and to PURGE, and to make them white, even to the time of the end." Again, in Daniel 12: 10 we read:"Many shall be purified, and made white, and tried; but the wicked shall do wickedly."

W. H. Hubbard writes:"The great tribulation is the chastening fires, over which the Lord sits as the refiner of silver, watching, guarding, these imperfect, unfit, unworthy, but loved ones, until the dross has been purged and they are ready to reign with Him and to 'offer unto the Lord an offering in righteousness.'" (Malachi 3:3)

While many agree that God chastens His own that go astray, yet they cannot see the tribulation as a time of chastening. Our Lord says concerning the Laodiceans,"As many as 1 love 1 chasten: be zealous therefore, and repent."

How much plainer can the Scriptures get?

The tribulation will serve as a time of trial for the endtime church that is plagued by worldliness, characterized by lukewarmness, beset with apostasy, and stained with uncleanness. Divorce and remarriage among professing Christians in opposition to God's Holy Word, along with immoral practices and immodest dress and behaviour must surely be dealt with as our Lord comes for a church that is "without spot or wrinkle or any such thing." (Ephesians 5:27)

God's promise is to keep the Philadelphia Church from this hour of trial because they have heeded God's Word and, patiently kept it. (Revelation 3:10)

As Dr. Joseph Hoffman Cohn observes: "Apparently, the Philadelphian and Laodicean churches are to exist contemporaneously during the closing days of the age; the church of Philadelphia being the faithful believers to whom is promised deliverance, and that of Laodicea, the apostate professors finally to be spued out."

Finally, evidence of one looking for His Lord's coming but left behind with unbelievers is clearly taught by Jesus. Concerning the servant that prepared not himself, our Lord taught that His coming will be at an hour when he is not aware, and will cut him in sunder, and will appoint him his portion with the UNBELIEVERS." (Luke 12:46)

This Scripture clearly teaches that if we don't prepare adequately we will be left behind with unbelievers. How careful we should be to heed these Scriptures. The Bible admonishes:"If we judge ourselves we would not be judged. But when we are judged, we are chastened of the Lord, that we should not be condemned with the world." (I Corinthians 11:31-32)

Today let us come to Christ and seek His forgiveness by repenting from all known sin. Let us renounce all the hidden things of dishonesty in our lives and with the power of the Holy Spirit, seek to be overcomers.

ERROR No. 2…That millions will be missing at the rapture.

Jude declares, quoting Enoch:"Behold the Lord cometh with TEN THOUSANDS of his saints…" (Jude 14) The amount of saints to be raptured may be so minimal so as not to be missed. If Enoch was a type of the rapture, and he was the only one taken, what right have we to expect to see "millions" raptured?

Yes, we admit it will be wonderful if millions will be raptured, but Enoch's reference to "TEN THOUSANDS" puts a limit to the number who will be caught up for that marriage supper, and later will reign with Christ. On the other hand, the number of those left behind to go through the tribulation is expressed as a "great multitude which no man could number." So we might question whether there will be millions missing!

ERROR No. 3...That all babies will be raptured.

The late C. M. Ward of REVIVAL TIME wrote: "Suddenly, 'in a moment, in the twinkling of an eye' (I Corinthians 15:52) there will be a planet without an infant." Says Dr. Ward, "It is inconceivable that 'little children' judged innocent - should be left behind to face the Great Tribulation..." I would hope Dr. Ward is correct.

Our Lord, in referring to the days of vengeance, declared: "Woe unto them that are with child, and to them that give suck, in those days!" Luke 21:22.

I am not dogmatic to declare that little children will be left behind at the rapture, but I do see the time of intense suffering coming upon the world as applicable to all except those found worthy to escape as judged by God's standards.

I am reminded in I Corinthians at children are protected in the event one of the parents is a believer, and are thus considered "holy." For we read: "The unbelieving husband is sanctified by the wife, and the unbelieving wife is sanctified by the husband: else were your children unclean; but now are they holy."

Thus, I see where children of a saved parent may be protected in the time of rapture. Otherwise, we offer little hope for unsaved infants who may share this endtime judgment along with their parents.

ERROR No. 4...That all believers are destined to be kings and priests.

While it is true that our Lord taught that faithfulness would be rewarded and depending upon the use of our "talents" we would reign over certain cities; yet it is understandable that surely there must be subjects to be ruled over, as well as kings and priests. (See Luke 19:16-19)

This reminds me of the time when as children we played

cowboys and Indians. If all wanted to be cowboys, then the game could not be played for some had to be the Indians.

So, the right to reign with Christ may depend upon certain accomplishments or attainments. As we read in 2 Timothy 2:12, "If we suffer, we shall also reign with him."

Now concerning the raptured group, in Revelation 5:9-10, it is specifically stated concerning these redeemed out of every kindred, and tongue, and people, and nation that they are "made unto our God kings and priests: and we shall reign on the earth."

However, concerning those who apparently missed the rapture, and who are seen going through the great tribulation, it is said they "are before the throne of God, and SERVE Him day and night in His temple." (Revelation 7:15)

Which would you sooner be—a KING and PRIEST, or a SERVANT? This, we believe, is what the Scripture means when it says we're to make our calling and election sure. We can remain a believer, or we can give up all to follow Christ and choose to be one of His disciples. In a sense we realize all will ultimately reign with Christ (Revelation 22:5) but see a difference between being a king and a servant.

ERROR No. 5…That the 144,000 sealed Israelites will win the "great multitude" in Revelation 7:14 to Christ during the tribulation period.

Even Dr. Howard C. Estep admits there are many Scriptural snags if you try to believe this theory. He calls such a belief a "traditional assumption, and it's not based wholly and completely upon the Word of God." I agree. The Jews will be hunted down, persecuted and killed during this "time of Jacob's trouble." The Jews which escape will no doubt be shut away in a place God has prepared for them which many believe to be the ancient stone city of Petra. I cannot visualize

Jews on street corners of the world winning converts as did the Apostle Paul, which is a current theory. As Dr. Estep concludes:"Therefore, logically and Scripturally, if the remnant of Israel, (the 144,000) are shut away during the last half of the 70th week of Daniel, how would they preach the Gospel during the Tribulation period?"

ERROR No. 6 ... That we need not be Holy to meet the Lord as Hebrews 12:14 declares.

Again, there are those who assume that the grace of God in salvation sees us justified and ready for the coming of the Lord. While we rejoice in the grace of God and full salvation yet we are reminded of Paul's letter to Titus wherein he writes: "For the grace of God that bringeth salvation hath appeared to all men, teaching us that, denying ungodliness and worldly lusts, we should live soberly, righteously, and godly, in this present world; looking for that blessed hope, and the glorious appearing of the great God and our Saviour Jesus Christ; who gave himself for us, that he might redeem us from all iniquity..." Titus 2:11-14

Jude also warns of those who turn the grace of God into lasciviousness (or loose, careless living). (Jude 4)

Jesus related how many will say in that day, "Lord, Lord, have we not prophesied in thy name? and in thy name have cast out devils? and in thy name done many wonderful works? And then (says Jesus) will I profess unto them, I never knew you: depart from me, ye that work iniquity." So you see our iniquity (sin) can keep us from being ready for the coming of the Lord.

For this reason the Scriptures emphasize: "Follow peace with all men, and holiness, without which no man shall see the Lord." Hebrews 12:14

Again, concerning those who meet the Lord, we read:

"Blessed and HOLY is he that hath part in the first resurrection." Revelation 20:6

We might add that when our Lord comes He will not divide men into "saved" and "unsaved" as we might think. Rather, He makes four separate distinctions according to Revelation 22:11-12. There are the unjust, the filthy, the righteous and the holy. To be ready for the rapture it would seem we must be among the righteous and the holy. What do you think?

ERROR No. 7...That God's Spirit will be withdrawn from the earth following the rapture and no one can be saved.

I don't want to convey the idea of a second chance, for if anyone rejects Christ now, it is doubtful that he will accept Him during the tribulation knowing the consequences that he may have to die for his faith. However, the Scriptures do indicate that Joel's prophecy concerning the outpouring of the Spirit is related to the time when "the sun shall be turned into darkness, and the moon into blood." And it is stated: "It shall come to pass, that whosoever shall call upon the name of the Lord shall be saved." Acts 2:20-21.

Thus, while we see the Holy Spirit withdrawn in those believers who are caught up at the time of the Rapture, we likewise see where God's Spirit is active upon the earth during the awful tribulation period. It is a case of "where sin abounds, grace doth also abound."

In fact, God sends His two witnesses that from them will flow the golden oil. (Zechariah 4:6, 14) (Revelation 11:3-4)

ERROR No. 8...That believers need not pray for Christ to return.

How wrong! Our Lord said: "Watch ye therefore, and pray always, that ye may be accounted worthy to escape all these things that shall come to pass, and to stand before the Son of man." Luke 21:36.

We're told Sam Rutherford knew how to pray for our Lord's coming. Here are several of his prayers:

"Oh, when will we meet? Oh, how long is it to the dawning of the marriage day? O sweet Jesus, take wide steps! O my Lord, come over mountains at one stride! O my Blessed, flee as a roe or young hart upon the mountains of separation! Oh, if He would fold the heavens together like an old cloak, and shovel time and days out of the way, and make ready in haste the Lamb's wife for her Husband!

"O fairest among the sons of men, why stayest Thou so long away? O heavens, move fast! O time, run, run, and hasten the marriage day, for love is tormented with delays! O angels, O seraphim who stand before Him, O blessed spirits who now see His face, set Him on high; for when ye have worn your harps in His praise, all is too little, and is nothing, to cast the smell of the praise of that fair flower, that fragrant Rose of Sharon, through many worlds!"

ERROR No. 9... That no preparation is needed to be ready for the rapture.

Again, this is a false assumption. After reminding us of the time when our Lord shall appear, John testifies: "And every man that hath this hope in him purifieth himself, even as he is pure." (I John 3:2-3)

John further conveys the idea that some believers will shrink back at our Lord's coming, unprepared to meet Him. He writes: "And now, little children, abide in him, that when he shall appear, we may have confidence, and not be ashamed before him at his coming." (I John 2:28) Vincent, referring to this passage, says: "The fundamental thought is that of separation and shrinking from God through the shame of conscious guilt."

Dr. Wuest similarly comments this translation might be rendered: "...whenever He is made visible, we may" not be made to shrink away from Him in shame at His coming and personal appearance." Dr. Wuest further maintains that this passage refers to the day when our Lord "comes from heaven into the atmosphere of this earth to catch out His Bride, the church."

When R. A. Torrey was asked, what constitutes readiness for the coming of the Lord, he replied: "Separation from the world's indulgence of the flesh, from the world's immersion in the affairs of this life, and intense daily earnestness in prayer."

Commenting on the need of readiness for Christ's coming, Dr. M. R. DeHaan wrote: "There is no greater incentive to holiness than the constant expectation of our Lord's return at any time."

ERROR No. 10...That the rapture is a gift included in our salvation and not a "crown" or "reward" for those who are ready.

From the previous Scriptures given, we can't help but wonder whether the "rapture is the reward of readiness!"

As Ira E. David notes: "We believe that the frequent exhortations in the Scriptures to watch, to be faithful, to be ready for Christ's coming, to live Spirit-filled lives, all suggest that translation is a reward."

The Apostle Paul said: "I press toward the mark for the prize of the high calling of God in Christ Jesus." The margin says "upward calling." Again Paul wrote: "If by any means I might attain unto the resurrection of the dead." (Philippians 3:11,14) What did he mean?

G. M. Pember comments: "Paul unmistakably affirms that these high privileges are a prize and not a gift, and are accessible only by the gate of the first resurrection—a gate through which, after all his sacrifices and labours and sufferings for Christ, he was not yet absolutely sure that he would be permitted to pass. Just before his death, however, it was graciously revealed to him that he was one of the approved...But, at the time when he was writing to the Philippians, he could not speak with such confidence."

Our Lord urged us saying:"Watch and pray always that ye may be accounted worthy to escape all these things that shall come to pass, and to stand before the son of man." (Luke 21:36) We're quick to reply that our worthiness will never save us, and this is true.

However, other Scriptures similarly sound a same call. Paul, writing to the Thessalonians, speaks of"being counted worthy of the kingdom of God." (II Thessalonians 1:5) Again, he declares concerning our Lord's coming-"We pray always for you, that our God would count you worthy of this calling..." (2 Thessalonians 1:11)

So, as W. H. Hubbard observes: "To escape the great tribulation and be able to stand before the Son of man, are not unconditioned gifts of love or grace, but rewards and privileges for those who. are accounted worthy of them."

CHAPTER 11

BE READY! A WARNING TO LUKEWARM CHRISTIANS!

It behooves us to be found ready whenever our Lord may come. However, the evidence is overwhelming that one of the purposes of the tribulation is for the chastening of lukewarm Laodiceans; whereas, the promise to Philadelphia believers is that of being kept from the hour of trial "to try them that dwell upon the earth."

Dr. Francis Schaeffer, author of THE CHURCH AT THE END OF THE 20TH CENTURY, sees an endtime Church where no gospel is preached, and likens this generation to that of ancient Israel which went whoring after idols.

Would it not appear that as we come to the close of this Laodicean Age that God is left with no choice but to weed out the chaff and then take the grain into the granary. This, then, we see as one of the purposes of the great tribulation. There must come a sifting time for those whose faith is shallow, lukewarm and indifferent.

For instance, years ago, we experienced "The Jesus Movement". It was "cool" to be a Christian. And many jumped aboard the bandwagon who saw Jesus as a revolutionary or superstar.

That a time of trial of men's faith is destined to come is a certainty. Our Lord Himself raised the question, "When the Son of man cometh shall he find faith on the earth?" The Apostle Paul spoke of those in the latter times who would "depart from the faith." (1 Timothy 4:1) Thus, there is coming this time of fiery trial at the end of this age for the purpose of purging: and purifying.

Malachi writes: "But who may abide the day of his coming? and who shall stand when he appeareth? for he is like a refiner's fire, and like fullers' soap." (Matthew 3:3) Fire and soap speak of purging and purifying. We read further: "And he shall sit as a refiner and purifier of silver." Ask any Bible theologian and you will be told that silver speaks of redemption. Thus, we see our Lord purifying those whom He has redeemed.

A silversmith was asked, "Do you sit as you carry on the process of refining silver?" He replied, "Yes, I must sit and my eyes must constantly watch the silver as it is being cleaned. Should the silver be exposed to the extreme heat for too long a time it would be damaged." On the other hand, the silversmith replied, "My work is complete and in good order when I can see my own image mirrored in the silver."

In view of the coming of the Lord we are told: "And every man that hath this hope in him purifieth himself, even as he is pure." (1 John 3:3)

But what if we fail to purify ourselves? Will we be left behind to go through the purifying judgment of the great tribulation?

Daniel, referring to the time of the end, writes: "Many shall be purified and made white, and tried; but the wicked shall do wickedly:" (Daniel 11:35)

That Laodicean believers will be spued out into the purging, purifying fires of the great tribulation is a Scriptural certainty. On the other hand, the promise to the believers who comprise the Philadelphia Church age which overlaps this period, is exemption from this trial of fire. For we read: "Because thou hast kept the word of my patience, I also will keep thee from the hour of temptation, which shall come upon all the world, to try them that dwell upon the earth." (Revelation 3:10)

Did you notice the purpose of this coming hour of testing is to "try them that dwell upon the earth"? The Great Tribulation is for evil doers and not for obedient disciples. As we read in Romans 2:9 where we find, "Tribulation and anguish, upon every soul of man that doeth evil, of the Jew first, and also of the Gentile."

Some see the tribulation period as being for Jews only—their time of trouble. But it will also be a testing time for lukewarm Laodiceans who profess faith in Christ but in works deny Him. Thus, through testing seen coming—a trial by fire—many will be purged and purified as silver.

As a matter of fact, in Revelation 7:14 we read of a great multitude which no man could number of whom it was said, "These are they which came out of great tribulation and have washed their robes, and made them white in the blood of the Lamb." As we see it, now is the time to come clean, forsake all known sin, and get ready for Christ's coming.

Does it not behoove us to be found living for Christ, obedient to His Word, sacrificial in our service, generous in our giving, fired up with a zeal, filled with the Holy Spirit, and ready for the rapture!

Now some evangelical Bible teachers tell us that when the Lord comes He will take some from the tavern and some from the theatre and together we will proceed to the marriage supper of the Lamb. There will be a stopping off place for a time of judgment after which we will all be ready for that glorious wedding day.

However, as I read the Bible, it appears that we must make preparation now. We are to "lay aside every weight and the sin which doth so easily beset us..." (Hebrews 12: 1)

In a time of serious affliction, the Lord showed me Hebrews 10:26, "For if we sin willfully after that we have received the knowledge of the truth, there remaineth no more sacrifice for sins, but a certain fearful looking for of judgment and fiery indignation which shall devour the adversaries." In other words, if we sin willfully Christ cannot go back and die every time we sin. While it is true that He willingly and gladly forgives, yet there comes an end to His patience and He allows chastening to come our way.

Remember, to the Laodiceans our Lord says: "As many as I love I rebuke and chasten!" (Revelation 3:19) Chastening is God's way of correcting His children. "For whom the Lord loveth, he chasteneth, and scourgeth every son whom he receiveth." (Hebrews 12:6) The purpose of chastening is said to be that of perfecting us spiritually, for we read: "Now no chastening for the present seemeth to be joyous, but grievous: nevertheless afterward it yieldeth the peaceable fruit of righteousness unto them which are exercised thereby."

Thus, the tribulation is a time of chastening for Laodiceans. It is a time of intense suffering-"as travail upon a woman with child" (1 Thessalonians 5:3) Mark refers to it as a time of great "affliction." What would be the purpose of this suffering? Again, we're reminded of the words of the Psalmist who said, "Before I was afflicted I went astray; but now have I kept thy word." (Psalm 119:67)

Some do not recognize suffering as bringing men to repentance. But Peter declares otherwise, saying: "He that hath suffered in the flesh hath ceased from sin..." (1 Peter 4:1)

A minister wrote that he did not always agree with us, but that "now it seems so clear to me that the Lord is coming for a Bride who is prepared, cleansed and obedient and that these are the ones who will reign with Him. What a new light this throws on suffering."

This is one of the reasons for the tribulation that will end this age. Through suffering great affliction, many will die as martyrs for their faith in Christ. That is how this age will end.

For this reason I believe God's purpose is to rapture the saints who have heeded this message and gotten the victory over sin through the shed blood of Christ and the power of the Holy Spirit. If the tribulation is for the purpose of purging, purifying—a time of trial—a period of chastening and affliction on account of sin, why should a born-again believer be subjected to this terrible ordeal if he is living victoriously over sin?

And, if not victorious over sin, may we be challenged to forsake every known sin..."to follow peace with all men, and holiness, without which no man shall see the Lord." (Hebrews 12:14)

Decide now to come to know Christ as Saviour and Master. Surrender to Him as your Lord. Allow Him to purify your heart by faith believing He can perfect what is lacking in your life and then keep you ready for His unannounced return.

Remember, He is the author and finisher of your faith. So lay claim to His promise that "He which hath begun a good work in you will perform it until the day of Jesus Christ." (Ephesians 1:6)

"And the very God of peace sanctify you wholly; and I pray God your whole spirit and soul and body be preserved blameless unto the coming of our Lord Jesus Christ." What an assignment I But remember, "Faithful is he that calleth you, who also will do it." (I Thessalonians 5:23-24)

CONCLUSION

This may be the day! ARE YOU READY?

Many will refuse to accept this message. They will claim the standard is too high, that no one can attain unto it. However, Peter speaks of an "abundant entrance" into the everlasting kingdom of our Lord Jesus Christ. Why consider getting to heaven by the skin of our teeth, or as by fire! Rather, if we are truly a part of the Bride of Christ we will be ready!

As we read, "Let us be glad and rejoice, and give honour to him: for the marriage of the Lamb is come, and HIS WIFE HATH MADE HERSELF READY. And to her was granted that she should be arrayed in fine linen, clean and white: for the fine linen is the righteousness of saints." (Revelation 19:7-8)

Incidentally, the Williams Translation says: "The linen signifies the upright deeds of God's people." Phillips says: "Such living is the righteous living of the saints."

So it is important how we live in view of Christ's coming.

May we make sure we know Christ as Saviour and Lord, and that we're found living for His soon coming. For He hath said: "Be ye therefore ready also, for in such an hour as ye think not, the Son of man cometh!"

An editorial in CHRISTIANITY TODAY relates how there is not the interest in our Lord's Coming as there should be. The magazine states: "Prior to World War I, many pulpits sounded forth the note of the possible imminent return of Jesus Christ to earth." Notes this magazine: "Since that time, eschatology has taken a back seat, and as a pulpit topic in the church the end time has given way to more mundane matters, such as feeding the hungry, preventing war, and binding up the wounds of the sick."

While we need to be concerned about the needs of the world about us, our interest in our Lord's Return should not wane but increase with each passing hour.

The editorial continues: "Paul wrote to Titus about 'awaiting our blessed hope, the appearing of the glory of our great God and Saviour Jesus Christ, who gave himself for us to redeem us from all iniquity. (2:13,14) Somehow the Church does not seem to be alight with this hope," notes this periodical. Indeed, how sadly true!

Dr. Claude A. Ries has cautioned: "The truth of the Second Coming of our Lord constantly reminds us that this earth is not our permanent dwelling place, that we are pilgrims here, and that we 'look for a city which hath foundations, whose builder and maker is God.' Therefore, we must hold lightly the things of this world, and all of earth's activities should be carried on with the eternal viewpoint ever in mind."

It is in view of this Blessed Hope of our Lord's soon appearing that we should realize that He who has called us to "be ready" will also keep us ready for that all-glorious day of rapture.

In 1 Thessalonians 5:23 we read, "And the very God of peace sanctify you wholly; and I pray God your whole spirit and soul and body be preserved blameless unto the coming of our Lord Jesus Christ."

What an assignment - for "spirit and soul and body" to be preserved blameless unto the coming of Jesus! But notice the next verse: "Faithful is he that calleth you, who also will do it!" Hallelujah!

This may be the day…are you ready?

"Therefore be ye also ready: for in such an hour as ye think not the Son of man cometh." (Matthew 24:44)

If you have any questions, comments, or have been encouraged by this book, please write:

Dr. Ray Brubaker
GOD'S NEWS BEHIND THE NEWS
P.O. BOX 10475
ST. PETERSBURG, FL 33733